First World War
and Army of Occupation
War Diary
France, Belgium and Germany

3 CAVALRY DIVISION
Headquarters, Branches and Services
General Staff Appendices to 1141
31 July 1916 - 7 November 1918

WO95/1142/2

The Naval & Military Press Ltd
www.nmarchive.com
Published in association with The National Archives

Published by

The Naval & Military Press Ltd

Unit 10 Ridgewood Industrial Park,

Uckfield, East Sussex,

TN22 5QE England

Tel: +44 (0) 1825 749494

www.naval-military-press.com

www.nmarchive.com

This diary has been reprinted in facsimile from the original. Any imperfections are inevitably reproduced and the quality may fall short of modern type and cartographic standards.

© Crown Copyright
Images reproduced by permission of The National Archives, London, England, 2015.

Contents

Document type	Place/Title	Date From	Date To
Miscellaneous	4		
Miscellaneous	6th Cavalry Brigade. Appendix I	31/07/1916	31/07/1916
Miscellaneous	March Table for August 1st.		
Miscellaneous	G.243/6. Appendix III.	01/08/1916	01/08/1916
Miscellaneous	March Table 2nd August, 1916		
Miscellaneous	7th Cavalry Brigade. Appendix II	01/08/1916	01/08/1916
Miscellaneous	6th Cavalry Brigade. Appendix IV.	03/08/1916	03/08/1916
Miscellaneous	March Table for 4th August 1916		
Miscellaneous	6th Cavalry Brigade. Appendix V	04/08/1916	04/08/1916
Miscellaneous	March Table for August 5th, 1916		
Miscellaneous	A Form. Messages And Signals. Appendix 6		
Miscellaneous	6th Cavalry Brigade. Appendix VI	06/08/1916	06/08/1916
Miscellaneous	3rd Field Squadron. R.E. Appendix VII	08/08/1916	08/08/1916
Miscellaneous	6th Cavalry Brigade. Appendix VIII	11/08/1916	11/08/1916
Miscellaneous	7th Cavalry Brigade (2). Appendix IX	12/08/1916	12/08/1916
Miscellaneous	Parties Detached From Units Of The Division On 13/8/16		
Miscellaneous	6th Cavalry Brigade. Appendix XI	18/08/1916	18/08/1916
Miscellaneous	8th Cavalry Brigade. Appendix XII	21/08/1916	21/08/1916
Miscellaneous	A Form. Messages And Signals. Appendix XIII		
Miscellaneous	6th Cavalry Bde. Appendix XIV.	20/08/1916	20/08/1916
Miscellaneous	6th Cavalry Brigade. Appendix XV	26/08/1918	26/08/1918
Miscellaneous	6th Cavalry Bde. Appendix XVI	28/08/1916	28/08/1916
Miscellaneous	Parties Detached From Units Of The Division During August 1916. Appendix XVII		
Miscellaneous	6th Cavalry Brigade Appendix I	09/08/1916	09/08/1916
Miscellaneous	March Table For 10th September, 1916		
Miscellaneous	6th Cavalry Bde. Appendix II	10/09/1916	10/09/1916
Miscellaneous	March Table-3rd Cavalry Division-September 11th		
Miscellaneous	6th Cavalry Bde. Appendix III	11/09/1916	11/09/1916
Miscellaneous	March Table-3rd Cavalry Division-September 12th 1916		
Miscellaneous	6th Cavalry Brigade. Appendix IV	13/09/1916	13/09/1916
Miscellaneous	March Table 3rd Cavalry Division-September 14th 1916		
Miscellaneous	6th Cavalry Bde. Appendix V	14/09/1916	14/09/1916
Miscellaneous	March Table-3rd Cavalry Division-15/9/16		
Miscellaneous	6th Cavalry Bde. Appendix VI	15/09/1916	15/09/1916
Miscellaneous	6th Cavalry Bde. Appendix VII	16/09/1918	16/09/1918
Miscellaneous	6th Cavalry Bde. Appendix VIII	21/09/1916	21/09/1916
Miscellaneous	March Table 3rd Cavalry Division-22nd September 1916		
Miscellaneous	6th Cavalry Bde. Appendix IX	22/09/1916	22/09/1916
Miscellaneous	March Table 3rd Cavalry Division-23rd September 1916		
Miscellaneous	6th Cavalry Bde. Appendix X	23/09/1916	23/09/1916
Miscellaneous	March Table 3rd Cavalry Division-24th September 1916		
Miscellaneous	7th Cav. Bde. Appendix 1	29/10/1916	29/10/1916
Miscellaneous	Divisional School Of Instruction. Appendix 2	26/10/1916	26/10/1916

Miscellaneous	Winter Training 1916-1917. Appendix 3	25/10/1916	25/10/1916
Miscellaneous	Divisional Anti-Gas School. Appendix 4	07/11/1918	07/11/1918
Miscellaneous	Courses At Anti-Gas School.		
Miscellaneous	Winter Training of Signal Services. Appx 5	06/11/1916	06/11/1916
Miscellaneous	7th Cavalry Brigade. Appendix 6	11/11/1916	11/11/1916
Miscellaneous	Issued Nov. 10th '16 Appendix 6		

Appendix I.   W.D.

G.243/5.

6th Cavalry Brigade.
7th Cavalry Brigade.
8th Cavalry Brigade.
C.R.H.A.
3rd Field Squadron R.E.
3rd Signal Squadron.   Chaplain.
No.7 L.A.Car Battery.   Field Cashier.
Ammunition Column.   Liaison Officer.
O.C. A.S.C.   Camp Commandant.
A.A & Q.M.G.   Capt. E.W. BAKER, ASC,
A.D.M.S.   8th Cav.Bde.Transport Officer.
A.D.V.S.   Fourth Army (for information).
A.P.M.   Reserve Army (for information).
D.A.D.O.S.

Reference - 1/100,000.

1. The Division will move in two marches to the ST. RIQUIER area on August 1st and 2nd, in accordance with attached March Tables.
   All troops of the Division will be west of AMIENS by 2 p.m. on August 1st, and north of the River SOMME by 12 noon on August 2nd.

2. All sick horses will be evacuated under arrangements to be made direct with Brigades by the A.D.V.S.

3. 'B' Echelon transport of the Division will be divisionalised and march under the orders of Captain E.W. BAKER, A.S.C., the Senior Brigade Transport Officer.

4. The following will move independently under orders to be issued by the officers concerned, direct to allotted billeting areas, so as not to interfere with the march of the Division :-

   No.7 L.A.Car Battery.)
   Supply Column.   )   by
   Ammunition Park.   )   A.A & Q.M.G.
   Dismounted men.   )

   Motor Ambulances.   )   by
   12th Sanitary Section.)   A.D.M.S.

5. Brigades will be accompanied by their Batteries, Field Ambulances, Mobile Veterinary Sections and 'A' Echelons.

6. All units will halt for one hour to water, at the appointed watering places shewn in March Table.

7. Divisional Headquarters will move to LE QUESNOY on August 1st.

8. Acknowledge.

                                        Lieutenant-Colonel,
                                        General Staff,
31/7/16.   3rd Cavalry Division.
P.S. March Table for August 2nd will be forwarded later.

March Table for AUGUST 1st.

Unit.	Starting Pt.	Time.	Route.	Billeting Area.	Remarks.
Divisional Ammunition Col.	T-roads N. of VECQUEMONT.	2 a.m.	AMIENS STN. - DREUIL - PICQUIGNY - SOUES - LE QUESNOY.	LE QUESNOY. (2½ miles W. of SOUES).	(a) To water in the neighbourhood of BREILLY. (b) Tail to be clear of PICQUIGNY by 10-30 a.m.
7th Cavalry Brigade.	Canal Bridge S. of CORBIE.	5 a.m.	N of VECQUEMONT - LAMOTTE - AMIENS STN. - BREILLY - FOURDRINOY.	CAVILLON - OISSY - RIENCOURT.	To water in the neighbourhood of DREUIL.
H.Q., R.H.A. Dvl.H.Q. details 3rd Signal Sqn.	T-roads N. of VECQUEMONT.	6-15 am 6-20 am 6-25 am	Follow the 7th Bde. to BREILLY - thence via PICQUIGNY - SOUES	LE QUESNOY (2½ miles W. of SOUES).	(To water in the neighbourhood of DREUIL after the 7th Bde. have finished, under orders of Adjt.RHA.
3rd Fd.Sqn.	- do -	6-30 am	Follow 3rd Sig.Sqn.	LE QUESNOY.	
6th Cavalry Brigade.	X-roads at double L of LA NEUVILLE.	6 a.m.	O. of DAOURS - VECQUEMONT - road just S. of AMIENS CITADELLE - thence N. of SOMME to LA CHAUSSEE - thence via PICQUIGNY - SOUES.	SOUES - LE HESGE.	To water in the neighbourhood of ARGOEUVES.
8th Cavalry Brigade.	- do -	6-45 am	Follow the 6th Bde. to PICQUIGNY, thence to CROUY.	ST.PIERRE-à-GOUY - CROUY - HANGEST.	To water in the neighbourhood of BERTRICOURT.
'B' Echelons *	T-roads N. of VECQUEMONT.	7-50 am	AMIENS STN. - DREUIL - BREILLY.	Each Bde transport to be diverted to Bde areas above in turn.	To water W. of AMIENS under orders of Capt.E.W.BAKER, A.S.C.

* Divisionalised in order of march of Brigades under Captain E.W.BAKER, A.S.C.

Appendix III

GENERAL STAFF 3rd CAVALRY DIVISION

8th Cavalry Brigade.
7th Cavalry Brigade.
8th Cavalry Brigade.
C.R.H.A.
3rd Field Sqdn: R.E.
3rd Signal Sqdn:
Ammunition Column.
O.C. A.S.C.
A.A. & Q.M.G.
A.D.M.S.
A.D.V.S.
A.P.M.

G.243/6.

D.A.D.O.S.
Chaplain C. of E.
Field Cashier.
Liaison Officer.
Camp Commandant.
Captain E.W. Baker, ASC,
    8th Cav. Bde. Transport Officer.

1. In continuation of my G.243/5 of the 31st July herewith March Table for August 2nd.

2. Brigades will water under their own arrangements, but they must inform all troops in rear when and where they intend to do so.

3. The A.P.M. will arrange to have control posts at the following places:-

    HANGEST.
    CONDE.
    LIERCOURT.
    FLIXECOURT.

Each post will rejoin Divisional H.Q. at YVRENCH after the tails of columns have passed.

4. Divisional H.Q. will move to YVRENCH on August 2nd.

5. Acknowledge.

1st August, 1916.

Lieut-Colonel.
G.S. 3rd Cavalry Division.

P.T.O.

MARCH TABLE 21st AUGUST, 1916.

	Starting Pt.		Route.	Billeting area.	Remarks.
8th Cav. Bde.	Rly. bridge at HANGEST.	5.0 am.	LOURDON - FLIXECOURT- AILLY - ST RIQUIER - L'ETIENCOURT.	NEUILLY l'hôpital - LE PLESSIEL - DRUCAT.	
6th Cav Bde.	W. exit of SOUES.	5.0 am.	AIRAINES - SOREL - LIERCOURT - PONT REMY - BUIGNY l'ABBÉ - VAUCHELLES.	NEUF MOULIN - CAOURS - MILLEN-COURT.	
7th Cav. Bde.	N. exit of SOUES.	6.0 am.	Same as for 8th Bde. up to ST RIQUIER.	ST RIQUIER - DRUGY.	
H.Q. R.H.A. Div.H.Q. details 3rd Sig. Sqn. 3rd Fd. Sqn.	X roads 1500 N. of LE QUES-NOY, on the CONDÉ road.	7.0 am. 7.5 am. 7.10" 7.15"	CONDÉ - La FOLIE (N. of SOREL) BRUCAMPS - DOMQUEUR - YVRENCH.	YVRENCH.	Head not to pass the FLIXECOURT - ST RIQUIER road at LA FOLIE till the tail of the 7th Bde.has passed
Div. Ammn. Col.	-do-	7.30 am	CONDÉ - La FOLIE (N. of Somme) - AILLY - ST RIQUIER.	ONEUX.	Not to pass La FOLIE till tail of 7th Bde.has passed
"B" Echelons of Bdes, (in order of march, 8, 6, 7). Divisionalised under Captain Baker, A.S.C.	HANGEST.	8.15 am	CONDÉ - LIERCOURT - PONT REMY - BUIGNY l'ABBÉ.	From BUIGNY Bdo transport to be diverted to Bdo areas.	Head not to pass CONDÉ till tail of Div. Ammn. Col. has passed.
"B" Echelons of Div. Troops in order of march as in Col 4. under senior N.C.O.	X Roads 1500 N. of LE QUES-NOY.	9.0 am	Same route as Div. troops, column 4.	YVRENCH.	Not to pass CONDÉ till tail of "B" Echelons of Bdes have passed.

Appendix II

War Diary

G. 253.

7th Cavalry Brigade.
7th Machine Gun Squadron. (2 copies).
3rd Field Squadron.   (2 copies).
A.A. & Q.M.G.
Reserve Army (for information).

✱✱✱✱✱✱✱✱✱✱✱✱✱✱✱✱✱✱✱✱✱✱✱

1. (a) In confirmation of orders issued verbally, the following will proceed by bus for duty under orders of Reserve Army.

    (b) 7th Machine Gun Squadron :-

        2 Officers (including Officer who went on to Reserve Army H.Q. this afternoon).
        2 Sergeants.
        2 Corporals.
        24 other ranks. (being detachments of 6 men per gun).
        4 Machine guns.
        3,500 rounds S.A.A. per gun in belt boxes.

    (c) 3rd Field Squadron R.E.:-

        1 Officer.
        20 other ranks.
        Sufficient tools for making machine gun emplacements and dug-outs.

2. 4 Busses will arrive at Divisional H.Q. at 7 a.m. tomorrow 2nd August when detachment 3rd Field Squadron will parade at Divisional H.Q.

3. After embussing detachment 3rd Field Squadron R.E. at LE QUESNOY, the 4 Busses will proceed to OISSY where party from 7th Machine Gun Squadron will be picked up (Note :- H.Q. 7th Machine Gun Squadron is in OISSY CHATEAU).

From OISSY busses will proceed to Reserve Army H.Q. at TOUTENCOURT where the Officer i/c Party will receive further instructions.

4. Rations for 2nd August will be taken.

                              Signed. E. de BURGH. Major,
                                G.S. 3rd Cavalry Division.

1/8/16.

War diary

Appendix IV

6th Cavalry Brigade.	Capt Baker
7th Cavalry Brigade.	
8th Cavalry Brigade.	A.D.V.S.
C.R.H.A.	A.P.M.
3rd Field Squadron, R.E.	D.A.D.O.S.
3rd Signal Squadron.	Chaplain.
Divisional Amm. Col.	Field Cashier.
O.C. A.S.C.	Liaison Officer.
A.A & Q.M.G.	Camp Commandant.
A.D.M.S.	IX Corps (for information).

1. The Division will move to FRUGES area on August 4th and 5th, in accordance with the attached March Tables.

    (March Table for August 5th will be forwarded later).

2. The following will move independently under orders to be issued by the undermentioned :-

    No.7 L.A.Car Battery.)
    Supply Column.   )
    Ammunition Park.   ) By A.A & Q.M.G.
    Reserve Park.   )
    Dismounted men.   )

    Motor Ambulances.   ) By
    12th Sanitary Section.) A.D.M.S.

3. Brigades and Divisional Troops will water under their own arrangements, informing all units in rear when and where they intend to do so.

4. The A.P.M. will place 2 control posts in CRECY.

5. Divisional Headquarters will move to LIGESCOURT on August 4th.

6. Acknowledge.

Lieutenant-Colonel,
General Staff,
3rd Cavalry Division.

5/8/16.

P.T.O

H.Q. ...LE for 4th August 1916.

Unit.	Starting Point.	Time.	Route.	Billeting Area.	Remarks.
6th Cavalry Brigade.	X-roads just N. of M of MILLEN- COURT.	5 a.m.	DOMVAST - MARCHEVILLE - CRECY - LIGESCOURT.	BOUSSENT - MAINTENAY - Gd. & Pt. PREAUX - ST.REMY aux-Bois.	
7th Cavalry Brigade.	N. exit of ST.RIQUIER.	6 a.m.	- do -	SAULCHOY - HEBE- COURT - ARGOULES - LE PETIT CHEMIN - DOMINOIS.	
8th Cavalry Brigade.	X-roads at S. end of CANCHY.	7-15 am.	MARCHEVILLE - CRECY - LIGESCOURT.	DOURIEZ - MOULMEL - ESTPLVAL - PONCHES.	
3rd Field Sqn.R.E.	N.E. exit from ONEUX.	6 a.m.	X-roads 1 mile S.E. of YVRENCH - NOYELLE - X-roads at E of FONTAINE-sur-MAYE - LE BOISLE.	DOMPIERRE.	
Divl. Amn. Column.	- do -	6-15 am.	- do -	DOMPIERRE.	
H.Q. R.H.A. Dvl.H.Q.details 3rd Sig.Sqn.	N.E. exit of YVRENCHEUX.	9 a.m.	NOYELLE - R of ESTREE - WADICOURT.	LIGESCOURT.	
'B' Echelon under orders of Capt.BAKER, A.S.C. (8th Bde. Transport Officer).					
6th Brigade.	X-roads 400 yds. S. of DOMVAST Church.	8-15 a.m.	(MARCHEVILLE -		1. Will be directed to Bde. areas at LIGES- COURT. 2. Capt.BAKER will assume command of 'B' Echs. at X-rds S.E. of MARCHE- VILLE.
7th Brigade.	- do -	8-25 am.	(CRECY -		
8th Brigade.	X-roads S.E. of MARCHEVILLE.	9 a.m.	(LIGESCOURT.		

Appendix V

War Diary

G.260/5.

6th Cavalry Brigade.
7th Cavalry Brigade.
8th Cavalry Brigade.
C.R.H.A.
3rd Field Squadron R.E.
3rd Signal Squadron.
Divl. Amm. Column.
O.C. A.S.C.
A.A & Q.M.G.
A.D.M.S.

A.D.V.S.
A.P.M.
D.A.D.O.S.
Chaplain.
Field Cashier.
Liaison Officer.
Camp Commandant.
IX Corps (for information).

---

1. In continuation of my G.260/2 of the 3rd instant, herewith March Table for August 5th.

2. 'B' Echelons will accompany their Brigades and move under orders of Brigades concerned.

3. Brigades will water under their own arrangements.

4. The A.P.M. will arrange to have 2 control posts in HESDIN, 1 at the northern exit and 1 at the southern exit. These posts will rejoin at FRUGES when last unit has passed through. The posts will see that columns are closed up when passing through HESDIN.

5. Divisional Headquarters will move to TRAMECOURT on August 5th.

3. Acknowledge.

4/8/16.

Lieutenant-Colonel,
General Staff,
3rd Cavalry Division.

P.T.O.

MARCH TABLE for August 5th, 1916.

Unit.	Starting point.	Time.	Route.	Billeting Area.	Remarks.
7th Brigade in two columns.	Eastern Column. X-roads 2000 yds N. of DOURIEZ.	5-30 a.m.	(GOUY-ST. ANDRÉ - E of (BEAURAINVILLE - EMBRY - (le Val du FRESNE.	(BOURTHES - Le GATELET (- ERGNY - RUMILLY (- VERCHOCQ - PETTY - (WICQUINGHEM - (MUQUELIERS.	
	Western Column. N.E. exit from SAULCHOY on ST. RÉMY-aux-BOIS road.	5-30 a.m.	(ST. RÉMY-aux-BOIS - Pt. (81 - pt. 86 - BEAURAIN- (VILLE STATION - MARESLA (- HUMBERT - HAUTINGHEN.		
8th Brigade.	X-roads in RAPECHY (S.E. of FORTEFONTAINE)	11 a.m.	GUIGNY - D of HESDIN.	TENEUR - ERIN - TILLY-CAPELLE - BLANGY - BLINGEL - AUCHY - GRIGNY.	ROLLENCOURT not to be occupied as a billeting area.
6th Brigade in two columns.	Eastern Column. ST. RÉMY-aux-BOIS.	7-30 a.m.	(GOUY-ST. ANDEL - MARESQUEL (- AUBIN-ST VAAST.	(LOISON - OFFIN - (HESMOND - LEBIEZ - (ROYON - SAINS-les-(FRESSIN - FRESSIN - (WAMBERCOURT - ((AVRON.	
	Western Column. X-roads N. of H of MAINTENAY.	7-50 a.m.	(BUIRE-le-SEC - E of (BEAURAINVILLE.		
3rd Field Sqn	DOMPIERRE.	7 a.m.	GUIGNY - HESDIN - FRESSIN.	CREQUY.	
Div.Amn.Col.	- do -	7-15 a.m.	GUIGNY - HESDIN - FRUGES.	COUPELLE - VIEILLE.	
H.Q. R.H.A. Div.H.Q.details. 3'd Signal Sqn.	(X-roads 300 (yds.S.E. of (LIGESCOURT.	8-15 a.m.	DOMPIERRE - GUIGNY - HESDIN - RUISSEAUVILLE.	CREQUY. H.Q.R.H.A. CREQUY. Div.H.Q. TRAMECOURT. Signals. FRUGES.	Each unit to branch off to billeting area in turn from the main HESDIN - FRUGES road.

"A" Form.
Army Form C. 2121.

MESSAGES AND SIGNALS.

Prefix...... Code......m.	Words	Charge	This message is on a/c of:	Recd. at......m.
Office of Origin and Service Instructions.	Sent		Service.	Date......
COPY.	At......m. To...... By......		Appendix 6. (Signature of "Franking Officer.")	From...... By......

TO	6th) 7th) Cavalry Brigades. 8th)	A.A.& Q.M.G. (for information).

Sender's Number. G.279/2.	Day of Month 7th.	In reply to Number	A A A

In continuation of my G.279/1 regarding snipers AAA Two busses will be at FRUGES at 4 p.m. tomorrow 8th AAA Parties from 6th and 7th Brigades will embus at MAIRIE in FRUGES at 4 p.m. proceeding there under Brigade arrangements AAA Busses will then proceed to X-roads 400 yards E. of v 2nd N in ANVIN reference map 1/100,000 where party from 8th Brigade will embus at 4-30 p.m. AAA Busses then proceed to H.Q. 64th Infantry Brigade in ARRAS where they should arrive at 8 p.m. AAA Each regiment will provide its sniping party with a telescope AAA Acknowledge AAA

From	3 C.D.
Place	
Time	8-15 p.m.

The above may be forwarded as now corrected

(Z) Sd/E. de Burgh, Major, G.S.

Appendix VI   G.279/1.

War diary

6th Cavalry Brigade.
7th Cavalry Brigade.
8th Cavalry Brigade.
A.A. & Q.M.G.

****

    The 21st Division have asked if we can let them have some trained snipers to work in the line with them; in consequence the following detachment from each Brigade will be prepared to proceed by bus on the morning of the 8th instant :-

      (1 Officer.
      (1 Sergeant or Corporal.
      (8 other ranks.

    Each man will take his telescopicsighted rifle with him, also unexpended portion of current day's rations.

    Further detailed orders will follow.

                Signed. A.E.PAGET. Lieut-Colonel.
                              General Staff.
6/8/16.   3rd Cavalry Division.

Appendix VII

No. G. 285.

3rd Field Squadron. R.E.
A.A. & Q.M.G. (for information).

****

You are required to provide a detachment of 56 other ranks, with a suitable proportion of officers, for the purpose of constructing O.P's for Corps Artillery. They will be attached to II Corps and will proceed by Motor Lorry tomorrow to AVELUY. Details regarding time of departure will be sent later.

O.C. Detachment will report at Town Majors' house AVELUY where guides from the artillery of the 12th and 49th Divisions will meet them.

40 other ranks are for the 12th Division and 16 other ranks are for the 49th Division.

2. Acknowledge.

8/8/16.

Signed. A. E. PAGET. Lieut-Colonel.
G.S. 3rd Cavalry Division.

6th Cavalry Brigade.
7th Cavalry Brigade.
8th Cavalry Brigade.
A.A. & Q.M.G.
3rd Signal Squadron.
O.C., A.S.C.
O.C., Detachment (Copy to be given him by 8th Brigade).
Reserve Army   (for information)
2nd Corps.   (-do-   )

1. The Division is required to detail a detachment of 500 other ranks for laying deep cables under the orders of the 2nd Corps (Reserve Army).
   The Detachment will be found as follows:-

From the 6th Bde.	From the 7th Bde.	From the 8th Bde.
1 Captain	1 Captain.	1 Captain.
3 Subalterns	3 Subalterns.	3 Subalterns.
166 Other ranks.	167 Other ranks.	167 Other ranks.

Officers' Servants, Cooks etc, will be detailed by Brigades in addition to above numbers.

2. In addition to the above the following Headquarters personnel will be found:-

A Lieut-Colonel to command   found by the 8th Brigade.
A Major as Second-in-Command   "   7th   "
An Officer to act as Adjutant   "   8th   "
   "   "   "   " Q.M.   "   6th   "
S.S.M. to act as R.S.M.   "   7th   "
S.Q.M.S. to act as Q.M.S.   "   6th   "
Officers' Servants as required.
   The O.C. will arrange to take with him from his own Regiment :-
         1 Clerk.
         1 Cook.
         2 Cyclists.

3. The 3rd Signal Squadron will detail one motor cyclist to report to the O.C. so soon as the party arrives in the II Corps area. Cyclist to call at Divisional Headquarters for orders before he leaves.

4. The Detachment will probably be employed in the above area for a week or 10 days.

5. The Detachment will move tomorrow 13th inst, in 30 Divisional Lorries as follows:-
   10 Lorries will be at each Brigade Headquarters at 9 a.m.
   Brigades will direct Lorries to pick up men at regimental rendezvous, each Brigade lorry party will then proceed independently to II Corps area - via HESDIN - FREVENT - DOULLENS ACHEUX - rendezvous for lorries in II Corps area will be notified later.

                                                          An

(2).

An officer will be in charge of each Brigade lorry party, who will be responsible for the route taken by the 10 lorries of his Brigade.

Lorries will return under orders to be issued by the A.A. & Q.M.G.

6. O.C., A.S.C. will detail:-

   1 Divisional Motor to be at 8th Brigade Headquarters at 10 a.m. to pick up the O.C., Adjutant and their servants.

   1 Divisional motor to be at 7th Brigade Headquarters at 9.30 a.m. to pick up the Second-in-Command and his servant, thence to call at 6th Brigade Headquarters to pick up the Quartermaster and his servant.

7. Rations for current day will be taken.
The A.A. & Q.M.G. will arrange to detail sufficient lorries to remain with the detachment for ration purposes.

8. Unless further orders are issued to the contrary the O.C. will call for orders at II Corps Headquarters at SENLIS about 12 noon.

9. Acknowledge.

12/8/16.

Lieutenant-Colonel
General Staff,
3rd Cavalry Division.

Appendix IX

War Diary

No. G. 253/11.

7th Cavalry Brigade (2)
8th   "   "   (2)
3rd Field Squadron.
A.A. & Q.M.G.
Lieut. Harsh 7th M.G.Sqdn.
Reserve Army (for information)

1. G.253/2 dated 7/8/16 is cancelled.

2. 8th M.G. Squadron will proceed by bus on 13th August for duty under Reserve Army. Following personnel will be taken:-
    6 Officers.
    1 Clerk.
    6 Sergeants.
    6 Corporals.
    72 Gunners.
    6 Servants.
    1 Cook.

Total 98.

All guns and 3500 rounds per gun in belt boxes will be taken.

3. Of the above, a detachment consisting of
    2 Officers.
    2 Sergeants.
    2 Corporals.
    24 Other Ranks.
    2 Servants.
    4 Machine Guns with 3500 rounds S.A.A. per gun in belt boxes.
will relieve a similar detachment of 7th Machine Gun Squadron now attached 49th Division.
The remainder will proceed to Reserve Army Headquarters at TOUTENCOURT, where Captain DRUMMOND will receive further orders.

4. Detachment 3rd Field Squadron now with 49th Division will be relieved by a similar detachment from 3rd Field Squadron at same time as above Machine Gun detachment and relieving party will take over tools of party relieved.

5. Eight busses will be at Headquarters 8th Machine Gun Squadron at AUCHY-les-Hesdin at 7 a.m. 13th August. Three of these busses will be allotted to party from 8th Machine Gun Squadron and 3rd Field Squadron proceeding to relieve detachments with 49th Division.
Remaining five are for 8th Machine Gun Squadron proceeding TOUTENCOURT.

P.T.O.

(2)

6. Both parties will embus at AUCHY-les-HESDIN at
7 a.m. and will proceed together to TOUTENCOURT whence
three busses with reliefs will go on to CRUCIFIX Corner
(W.11.d.9.1.) where they will debus. They will be met
there by guides from the detachment now in the trenches.
   These three busses will remain at CRUCIFIX Corner
until arrival of party relieved, and will then convey them
back to billets as under:-
   (a) 3rd Field Squadron R.E.   TORCY.
   (b) 7th Machine Gun Squadron   AIX-en-ERGNY.

7. Remainder of 8th Machine Gun Squadron in 5 busses
will debus at TOUTENCOURT where they will billet. O.C.
will report to Town Major for billets.

8. Rations for current day will be taken.

9. Relieving party from 3rd Field Squadron will move
under their own arrangements so as to reach AUCHY by 7
a.m. where they will embus.

10. A divisional car will be at AUCHY at 7 a.m. and
will be available to take on representatives of 8th
Machine Gun Squadron and 3rd Field Squadron to CRUCIFIX
Corner.

11. Acknowledge.

                                         Major,
                              General Staff,
                                 3rd Cavalry Division.
12/8/16

Appendix 10

PARTIES DETACHED FROM UNITS OF THE DIVISION ON 13/8/16.

Unit.	Strength. Officers.	Strength. O.R.	Under Whom.	Work being done.	Date when commenced.	Remarks.
3rd Field Sqn.	1	20	Reserve Army.	Making machine gun emplacements and dug-outs.	2/8/16.	
7th Cav. Bde.	Lt.Graham.	C.of H.Mackrintosh 2nd Life Gds.	21st Dvn.School.	Sniping Instructors.	7/8/16.	
6th Cav. Bde.	1	10	) 64th Bde.	Snipers in front line.	8/8/16.	
7th Cav. Bde.	1	10	) 21st Dvn.			
8th Cav. Bde.	1	10	)			
(3rd Field Sqn.	2	40	12th Division. 49th Division.	Constructing O.P's. for II Corps Artillery.	) 9/8/16.	
(6th Cav. Bde.		16	3rd Fd. Sqn.	Assisting grooming horses.	)	
6th Cav. Bde.	4	166	)			H.Q. personnel -
7th Cav. Bde.	4	167.	) II Corps.	Laying deep cables.	13/8/16.	4 offrs. & 6 O.R.
8th Cav. Bde.	4	167	)			Servants in addition as required.
3rd Sig. Sqn.		1 (D.R).				
A.D.M.S.	Sufficient medical personnel.					
8th Machine Gun Squadron.	6	92	Reserve Army.	Duty in front line.	13/8/16.	Dismounted men of 8th Cav. Bde. to look after horses of 8th M.G. Squadron.

Appendix XI   W.D.

G.279/8.

6th Cavalry Brigade.   (3 copies).
7th Cavalry Brigade.   (3 copies).
8th Cavalry Brigade.   (3 copies).
A.A & Q.M.G.   (2 copies - 1 for N.C.O. i/c lorries).
21st Division.   (for information).

Detachment of snipers now with 21st Division will be relieved by detachments of same composition from each Brigade as follows :-

1. Incoming snipers will proceed in 3rd Cavalry Division lorries to 110th Brigade H.Q., Place ST.CROIX, ARRAS, so as to arrive there at 9-30 p.m. August 20th. Lorries must not enter ARRAS by daylight.
Detachments of 6th and 8th Brigades will be met there by representatives of 62nd and 64th Brigades respectively; 7th Cavalry Brigade will be attached to 110th Brigade.

2. Incoming snipers will be taken up to the posts already occupied by present Cavalry snipers and both parties will remain at these posts together throughout the 21st and 22nd August.

3. Outgoing snipers will collect at 110th Brigade H.Q. by 9-30 p.m. on 22nd, where same lorries will meet them and convey them back to permanent billets.

4. Relieving party will take over telescopic rifles and telescopes of party relieved.
Relieving party will take rations for 21st with them.

5. One lorry per Brigade will be at :-
    H.Q. 6th Cavalry Brigade.........1-30 p.m.
    H.Q. 7th Cavalry Brigade.........1-30 p.m.
    H.Q. 8th Cavalry Brigade.........3-30 p.m.,
where detachments will embus.

They will then proceed to the rendezvous at X-roads 400 yards E. of second N in ANVIN by 4-30 p.m.
From this rendezvous the three lorries will proceed together to H.Q. 110th Brigade., Place ST.CROIX, ARRAS, so as to arrive there at 9-30 p.m.

6. After delivering snipers in ARRAS, lorries will report to 21st Division H.Q. at DUISANS where they will be shown where they can remain during August 21st and 22nd.
N.C.O. in charge of lorries will have his lorries at H.Q. 110th Brigade at 9-30 p.m. on 22nd to convey back outgoing parties to permanent billets. Same lorries originally allotted to each Brigade will bring back the detachment of same Brigade by same route as on outward journey.

7. The Officer proceeding in charge of each Brigade party will be provided with two copies of this order; one being for the officer he relieves.

8. Brigades will arrange for meeting parties on their return.

9. Acknowledge.

Major,
General Staff,
3rd Cavalry Dvn.

18/8/16.

Appendix XII

G.325/4.

8th Cavalry Brigade.
3rd Field Squadron R.E.
A.A & Q.M.G.
XIII Corps (for information).
Reserve Army (for information).
----

1. The XIII Corps require a working party of 1 officer and 50 "other ranks" with a small R.E. personnel, for the construction of entraining and detraining places at CANDAS.

   This party will be attached to the R.F.C. for billeting and rations.

2. The 8th Brigade will provide the working party of 1 officer and 50 "other ranks".

   The 3rd Field Squadron will provide 1 officer and 2 N.C.Os the officer being responsible for supervising the work and for issuing orders to the Officer Commanding the Working Party.

3. The party will proceed to CANDAS in 3 supply lorries on Tuesday, August 22nd. The A.A & Q.M.G. will arrange to have the lorries at 8th Brigade Headquarters at 9-30 a.m. on 22nd instant. A.A & Q.M.G. will also arrange to send the officer and 2 N.C.Os. of 3rd Field Squadron R.E. to 8th Brigade Headquarters by that hour.

4. Party will take rations for 22nd.

5. The N.C.O. in charge of lorries will proceed via ST.POL, FREVENT and DOULLENS to CANDAS, as soon as lorries are loaded, and will return after leaving party there.

6. The Officer Commanding the Working Party will report on arrival at CANDAS to O.C. No.2 Aircraft Depot, R.F.C.

21/8/16.

Major,
General Staff,
3rd Cavalry Division.

"A" Form.
MESSAGES AND SIGNALS.

Army Form C. 2121.

COPY.

Priority.

TO: 6th)
7th) Cavalry Brigades.   A.A & Q.M.G.
8th)

Sender's Number.	Day of Month.	In reply to Number.	AAA
G.305/17.	23rd.		

Reserve Army require every possible dismounted man to be sent tomorrow to join party now at BOUZINCOURT AAA Following orders are in confirmation of telephonic orders AAA Two lorries for 6th Brigade will be at Headquarters 3rd Dragoon Guards at 9 a.m. tomorrow AAA Four lorries for 7th Brigade and three lorries for 8th Brigade will be at Headquarters of respective brigades at 9 a.m. AAA Lorries of each Brigade will pick up parties and proceed independently via FREVENT - DOULLENS - ACHEUX to BOUZINCOURT where they will report to Headquarters 3rd Cavalry Division Digging Party near Church AAA Rations for current day will be taken AAA Lorries will return after dropping parties AAA Numbers of parties will be 30 from 6th Brigade, 72 from 7th Brigade and 45 from 8th Brigade AAA

From: 3 C.D.
Place:
Time: 8-30 p.m.

(Z) Sd/E. de BURGH, Major, GS.

Appendix XIV.

W.D.

G.253/21.

6th Cavalry Bde. (2).
A.A. & Q.M.G.
II Corps (for information).
Reserve Army (for information).
----

1. Following orders are in confirmation of my G.253/19.

2. 6th Machine Gun Squadron will proceed in Divisional lorries on 27th August for duty under II Corps.

   Following personnel will be taken :-

        6 officers.
        1 clerk.
        8 Sergeants.
        8 Corporals.
        72 gunners.
        6 servants.
        1 cook.
        ─────────
        96
        ═════════

   All guns and 3,500 rounds per gun in belt boxes will be taken.

3. 7 Lorries will be at Headquarters 6th Machine Gun Squadron CAVRON-ST.MARTIN at 9 a.m. on 27th.

   After picking up party, lorries will proceed via PREVENT - DOULLENS and ACHEUX to BOUZINCOURT.

4. A Divisional car will be at Headquarters 6th Machine Gun Squadron at 9 a.m. to take O.C. Squadron on to II Corps H.Q. in SENLIS, where he will report for instructions.

   He will meet his Squadron on their arrival at BOUZINCOURT.

5. Acknowledge.

                                            Major,
                                        General Staff,
                                    3rd Cavalry Division.

26/8/16.

appendix XV. W.D.

6th Cavalry Brigade.
7th Cavalry Brigade.
8th Cavalry Brigade.
A.A & Q.M.G.
II Corps (for information).

1. The officers of the 1/1 Yorkshire Dragoons (Corps Cavalry Regiment with II Corps) will be attached to the Division in three different parties, for a period of 1 week each, as follows :-

To 6th Brigade. 1st Party.	To 7th Brigade. 2nd Party.	To 8th Brigade. 3rd Party.
Major J.L. Ingham.	Major E. Wood.	Lt.Col.W.McK.Smith.
Captain J.R. Foster.	Lieut. L.P. Clay.	Capt. R. Thompson.
Lieut. B.A.L. Green.	" S. St.M. Delius.	" G.J. Hirst.
" W.E.R. Fowler.	" E. Tinker.	Lt. D.C. Long.
" G.L. Clark.	2/Lt. M. Sheppard.	2/Lt.M.W. Hudson.
2/Lt. R.R. Beilby.	" J. Robins.	" G. Hesketh.
" H.B. Chamberlin.	" A.F. Bates.	Lt. W.R.P. Warde-Aldam.
" D.F. Porter.	" D.E. Worthington.	2/Lt.H.F.B. Stephenson.
(Aug.28th – Sept.4th)	(Sept 4th – Sept.11th)	(Sept 11th – 18th)

The parties will arrive respectively on August 28th, September 4th and 11th and leave respectively on September 4th, 11th and 18th.

2. Brigades will arrange to attach these officers as follows – C.O. and 2nd-in-Command to H.Q. of Regiment, Squadron Leaders to H.Q. of a Squadron, Subalterns to a troop.

3. II Corps will arrange to send the parties in turn to report to Brigade Headquarters as follows :-

1st Party to 6th Brigade H.Q. EMBRY on August 28th.
2nd "   " 7th   "   " " BUCQUELIERS on September 4th.
3rd "   " 8th   "   " " ERIN on September 11th.

4. The officers concerned will attend all tactical exercises carried out during their period of attachment, and should also carry out duties with troops whenever possible.

The Reserve Army Commander desires that every effort should be made to render the training as practical and as valuable as possible.

A.C.Pask.
Lieutenant-Colonel,
General Staff,
3rd Cavalry Division.

28/8/16.

Appendix XVI W. Diary

G.305/27.

6th Cavalry Bde.	Major Hon. E. WYNDHAM,
7th Cavalry Bde.	Cdg. 3 C.D. Detachment.
8th Cavalry Bde.	II Corps }
O.C. A.S.C.	Reserve Army } for information.
3rd Signal Sqn.	1 Anzac Corps }
A.A & Q.M.G.	
A.D.M.S.	

---

1. The 3rd Cavalry Division detachment of 500 men now working under the Reserve Army will be relieved on the 31st August and 1st September by a similar detachment as follows:-

August 31st.

6th Brigade.	7th Brigade.	8th Brigade.
2 officers.	4 officers.	2 officers.
80 other ranks.	167 other ranks.	80 other ranks.

September 1st.

6th Brigade.	7th Brigade.	8th Brigade.
2 officers.		2 officers.
86 other ranks.	Nil.	87 other ranks.

Officers' servants, cooks, orderlies, etc. will be detailed by Brigades in addition to above numbers.

Note - In each Brigade party, the senior officer must be a Captain.

2. In addition to the above, the following Headquarters personnel will be found by Brigades concerned and will relieve the present Headquarters on August 31st :-

A Major to command by the 6th Brigade.
An Officer to act as Adjutant by the 6th Brigade.
"   "   " "   " Qr. Mr.   "   " 7th   "
S.S.M. to act as R.S.M.   "   " 8th   "
S.Q.M.S. "   "   " Q.M.S.   "   "   "   "

The O.C. will arrange to take with him from his own Regiment :-

1 Clerk.
1 Cook.
2 Cyclists.

3. The 3rd Signal Squadron will continue to employ a motor cyclist with the detachment.

4. The medical personnel will not be relieved.

5.

2.

5.   The relieving detachment will move in Divisional lorries, who will report as follows :-

<u>August 30th</u>.   12 lorries will be at H.Q. 7th Brigade at 5 p.m., to be distributed over-night to regimental billeting areas.

6 lorries will be at H.Q. 6th and 8th Brigades respectively at 5 p.m., to be distributed over-night to regimental billeting areas.

Brigade lorry parties will proceed independently to BOUZINCOURT on August 31st, leaving 7 a.m.

<u>August 31st</u>.   6 lorries will be at H.Q. 6th and 8th Brigades respectively at 5 p.m., to be distributed over-night to regimental billeting areas.

Brigade lorry parties will proceed independently to BOUZINCOURT on September 1st, leaving 7 a.m.

<u>Route for lorries</u> - HESDIN - FREVENT - DOULLENS - MARIEUX - ACHEUX.

An officer will be in charge of each Brigade lorry party who will be responsible for marshalling the lorries and for the correct route.

6.   Major Hon. E. WYNDHAM, 1st Life Guards, will be responsible for arranging for the return of the troops who have been relieved, and for directing the Brigade lorry parties back to Brigade billeting areas.

7.   The 6th Brigade will arrange to send the O.C. and Adjutant by motor to BOUZINCOURT, on 31st.

8.   Rations for the current day will be taken.

9.   Acknowledge.

[signature]

Lieutenant-Colonel,
General Staff,
3rd Cavalry Division.

29/8/16.

Appendix XVII

PARTIES DETACHED FROM UNITS OF THE DIVISION DURING AUGUST 1916.

Unit.	Strength. Offrs.	Strength. O.R.	Under Whom.	Work being done.	Date commenced.	Remarks.
3rd Field Sqn.	1	20	Reserve Army.	M.G. emplacements & dug-outs.	2/8/16.	
7th Cav. Bde.	1	1	21st Dvn. School.	Sniping Instructors.	7/8/16.	Lieut.Graham & C.of H. Mackintosh, 2/LG.
6th Cav. Bde.	1	10)	64th Inf. Bde.	Snipers in front line.	8/8/16	Parties relieved 21/22nd August.
7th	1	10)				
8th	1	10)	21st Division.			
3rd Field Sqn.	2	40	12th Division. }	Constructing O.Ps. for II Corps Artillery.	9/8/16.	
		16	49th Division. }		9/8/16.	
6th Cav. Bde.		40	3rd Field Sqn.	Assisting grooming horses.	9/8/16.	
6th Cav. Bde.	4	166	II Corps.	Laying deep cables, &c.	13/8/16.	H.Q. personnel - 4 officers, 6 O.R. Servants in addition as required.
7th Cav. Bde.	4	167				
8th Cav. Bde.	4	167				
3rd Sig. Sqn.		1 D.R				
A.D.M.S.		Sufficient medical personnel.				
8th M.G. Sqn.	6	92	Reserve Army.	Duty in front line.	13/8/16.	Dismounted men, 8th Cav. Bde. to look after M.G. Sqn. horses.
8th Cav. Bde.	1	50)	XIII Corps.	Constructing entraining & detraining places at CANDAS.	22/8/16.	Moved to BOUZINCOURT 24/8/16.
3rd Field Sqn.	1	2)				
6th Cav. Bde.)	1	30	II Corps.	Join diggers at BOUZINCOURT.	24/8/16.	
7th Cav. Bde.}		72				
8th Cav. Bde.}		45				
5th M.G. Sqn.	7	94	II Corps.	Duty in front line.	27/8/16.	In relief of 8th M.G. Sqn.(a)
6th Cav. Bde.	4	166)	II Corps.	Laying deep cables &c.	31/8/16.	In relief of similar party above.
7th Cav. Bde.	4	167)			1/9/16.	* Original party as above remained.
8th Cav. Bde.	4	167)				
3rd Sig. Sqn.		1 D.R)				
A.D.M.S.						

War Diary

Appendix I

6th Cavalry Brigade.   D.A.D.O.S.
7th Cavalry Brigade.   Chaplain.
8th Cavalry Brigade.   Field Cashier.
3rd Field Sqdn.   Liaison Officer.
3rd Signal Sqdn.   Claims Officer.
No.7. L.A.C.Battery.   Camp Commandant
C.R.H.A.   A.D.C.
Divl. Ammn. Column.   A.A.& Q.M.G.
A.D.M.S.   Cavalry Corps   (for information.)
A.D.V.S.   Reserve Army   -do-
A.P.M.   Third Army.   -do-
O.C., A.S.C.

1. The Division will march on September 10th to a billetting area on the AUTHIE River between ROUSSENT and DOMPIERRE in accordance with the attached March table.
   The March will be continued on the 11th, 12th and 13th September.

2. (a) "B" Echelons will accompany their Brigades.

   (b) The following units will not move on the 10th:-
       No. 7. Light Armoured Car Battery.
       Ammunition Park.
       Reserve Park.
       3rd Signal Squadron (less Horse transport)
       Dismounted party.
       Motor Ambulances (except those detailed by the A.D.M.S. to accompany Brigades).
   Orders concerning the move of these Units will be issued later.

3. All sick horses will be evacuated under arrangements to be made direct with Brigades by the A.D.V.S..

4. Divisional Headquarters will remain at TRAMECOURT till the morning of the 11th inst.

9th Sept. 1916.

Lieutenant-Colonel.
General Staff,
3rd Cavalry Division.

MARCH TABLE for 10th September, 1916.

UNIT	STARTING PLACE.	TIME	ROUTE	BILLETING AREA	REMARKS.
7th Brigade	Under Brigade Arrangements.	Under Brigade Arrangements.	Any roads West of and inclusive of the MANINGHEM-ST MICHEL ST DENOEUX-HAREM LA BEAURAINVILLE Station - ST REMY aux Bois road.	ROUSSENT-MAINTENAY -ST REMY aux Bois - GRAND PREAUX -PETIT PREAUX.	7th Bde will give 6th Bde. a copy of their orders
6th Brigade.	Under Brigade Arrangements.	Under Brigade Arrangements.	(a). B of BEAURAINVILLE - GOUY - ST ANDRE - (b) AUBIN ST VAAST - LABUS - ST JOSSE.	ARGOULES-le Petit CHENIN -DOMINOIS- SAULCHOY.	6th Bde. will give 7th Bde. a copy their orders.
8th Brigade.	Under Brigade Arrangements.	Under Brigade Arrangements.	(a). HESDIN-MOURIEZ- TORTEFONTAINE -MARCONNE PONCHES-LIGESCOURT -GUIGNY (b) HESDIN- -DOMPIERRE.	DOURIEZ-ESTRUVAL PONCHES-LIGESCOURT BOULMER-RAPECHY.	Head of the Bde not to pass HESDIN before 1 p.m.
3rd Field Squadron.	TORCY.	8 a.m.	FRESSIN-HESDIN- GUIGNY.	DOMPIERRE.	To arrange with 6th Bde about passing through FRESSIN
Divl. Amm. Column.	COUPELLE-VIEILLE	7.30 a.m.	FRUGES-HESDIN- GUIGNY.	DOMPIERRE	
H.Q., R.H.A. Div.H.Q.Details. Signal Squadron (less Motor transport) To march under orders of Adjutant R.H.A.	X roads just N.E. of Y of LE PLOUY	9.30 a.m.	-ditto- HESDIN - GUIGNY	DOMPIERRE	

Appendix II

War Diary

G.377/3.

6th Cavalry Bde.	O.C. A.S.C.
7th Cavalry Bde.	D.A.D.O.S.
8th Cavalry Bde.	Chaplain.
3rd Field Sqn.	Field Cashier.
3rd Signal Sqn.	Liaison Officer.
No.7 L.A. Cars.	Camp Commandant.
C.R.H.A.	A.D.C.
Div. Amm. Col.	A.A & Q.M.G.
A.D.M.S.	Cavalry Corps
A.D.V.S.	Reserve Army } for information.
A.P.M.	Third Army

---

1. The Division will march on September 11th to a billeting area north-east of ABBEVILLE, in accordance with March Table overleaf.

    The march will be continued on the 12th, 13th and 14th September.

2. (a) 'B' Echelons will march under orders of Brigades.

    (b) The following units will move under separate orders to be issued by the A.A & Q.M.G. :-

    Ammunition Park.
    12th Sanitary Section.
    Reserve Park.
    Dismounted party.

    (c) No.7 Light Armoured Car Battery and Motor Ambulances (except those with Brigades) will move on 11th in accordance with March Table overleaf.

3. Divisional Headquarters will move to MAISON-PONTHIEU on the morning of the 11th September.

4. Acknowledge.

Note:- The 1st Indian Cavalry Division will not now be clear of the new area before 2 pm

Lieutenant-Colonel,
General Staff,
3rd Cavalry Division.

10/9/16.

MARCH TABLE - 3rd Cavalry Division - September 11th.

Unit.	Starting Point.	Time.	Route.	Billeting Area.	Remarks.
H.Q. R.H.A., Dvl. H.Q. details, Signal Sqn. (less motor transport) under orders of Adjutant R.H.A.	Road and railway crossing just S.E. of DOMPIERRE.	8 a.m. 12 noon	LE BOISLE - BOUFFLERS - GUESCHARD - MAISON-PONTHIEU.	CONTEVILLE.	
3rd Field Sqn. R.E.	ditto.	12-15 p.m.	ditto.	ditto.	
Divl. Amn. Column.	ditto.	12-30 p.m.	ditto.	ditto.	
8th Cavalry Bde.	(a) LIGESCOURT. (b) DOMPIERRE.	1 p.m. 3 p.m.	(a) LIGESCOURT - CRÉCY - DOMVAST - LILLERCOURT. (b) DOMPIERRE - WADICOURT - R of ESTRÉES - NOYELLE-er-CHAUSSÉE - GAPENNES - ST. RIQUIER.	ST. RIQUIER - DRUGY - NEUF-MOULIN - CAOURS.	
6th Cavalry Bde.	(a) 6 cross-roads just S. of LE PETIT CHEMIN. (b) 4 cross-roads 500 yds. S.W. of DOURIEZ.	2 p.m. 4 p.m.	(a) VIRONCHAUX - W. end of CRÉCY - FOREST - L'ABBAYE. (b) LIGESCOURT - E. end of CRÉCY - X-roads 1000 yds. S.E. of MARCHEVILLE - NOYELLE-PLESSIEL - DRUCAT - MILLENCOURT - CANCHY.	CANCHY - NEUILLY-l'Hôpital - LE PLESSIEL - DRUCAT - MILLENCOURT.	
7th Cavalry Bde.	(a) SAULCHOY. (b) ARGOULES.	3 p.m. 4 p.m.	(a) DOMPIERRE - WADICOURT - ESTRÉES. (b) LIGESCOURT - CRÉCY - DOMVAST.	BRAILLY - NOYELLE-er-CHAUSSÉE - GAPENNES - ARGENVILLERS - DOMVAST.	
Dvl. H.Q. details at FRUGES & TRAMECOURT.	Starting Point and time to be arranged by Camp Commandant.		HESDIN - LE BOISLE - GUESCHARD.	MAISON-PONTHIEU - GUESCHARD.	Must not pass Gueschart before 2 p.m.

Motor Transport of Signal Squadron to move direct to MAISON-PONTHIEU v♦♦ HESDIN and LE BOISLE. *Must not pass these before 2 pm*

No.7 Light Armoured Car Battery to move under orders of O.C. to billets at NEUILLY-le-DIEN via HESDIN, LE BOISLE and GUESCHART, but not to pass LE BOISLE before 12 a.m. *2 pm*

Motor Ambulances to move under orders of A.D.M.S. via same route as Armoured Cars and billet as ordered by A.D.M.S. at either GUESCHART or MAISON-PONTHIEU. *Must not pass le BOISLE before 2 pm*

Appendix III

War Diary

GENERAL STAFF No. G.377/4. 3rd CAVALRY DIVISION

```
6th Cavalry Bde.      O.C. A.S.C.
7th Cavalry Bde.      D.A.D.O.S.
8th Cavalry Bde.      Chaplain.
3rd Field Sqn.        Field Cashier.
3rd Signal Sqn.       Camp Commandant.
No.7 L.A. Cars.       A.D.C.
C.R.H.A.              A.A & Q.M.G.
Divl. Amm. Col.       Liaison Officer.
A.D.M.S.              Cavalry Corps  )
A.D.V.S.              Fourth Army    ) for information.
A.P.M.                X Corps        )
```

---

1. The Division will continue its march on September 12th from the ST.RIQUIER area to an area north of the SOMME between YZEUX and ARGOEUVES.

    The Division will remain in the above area for the nights 12th/13th and 13th/14th, continuing the march on the 14th to Y area S.W. of VECQUEMONT.

2. (a) 'B' Echelons will march under orders of Brigades.

    (b) Following units will move under orders to be issued by A.A & Q.M.G. :-

    Ammunition Park.
    12th Sanitary Section.
    Reserve Park.

3. Divisional Headquarters will move to BELLOY-sur-SOMME on morning of 12th instant.

4. Acknowledge.

11/9/18.

Lieutenant-Colonel,
General Staff,
3rd Cavalry Division.

MARCH TABLE - 3rd CAVALRY DIVISION - September 12th 1916.

Unit.	Starting Pt.	Time.	Route.	Billeting Area.	Remarks.
6th Brigade.	CAOURS.	9-30 a.m.	VAUCHELLES - EPAGNE - PONT REMY - DUNCQ - thence main road S. of the SOMME to PICQUIGNY. Any route N. of the Somme	LA CHAUSSEE.	Head of the Bde. not to cross to the N. bank of the SOMME at LA CHAUSSEE till tail of the 8th Bde has passed.
8th Brigade.	YAUCOURT.	9 a.m.	AILLY - FLIXECOURT - LA CHAUSSEE.	ST.SAUVEUR ARGOEUVES.	
7th Brigade.	ST.RIQUIER.	10 a.m.	Follow the 8th Bde.	YZEUX.	(a) Fighting troops of 7th Bde can pass 'B' Ech. of 8th Bde on the march. (b) 7th Bde will leave a man at LA FOLIE X-roads till Dvl.H.Q. details reach that point.
Dvl. H.Q. details 3rd Sig. Sqn. under orders of O.C. 3rd Sig.Sqn.	AILSON-PONTHIEU.	15 a.m. 10-5 a.m.	YVRENCH - X-roads just S.E. of the S of St OUEN COULONVILLERS - AILSON- ROLLAND - GORENFLOS BRUCAMPS - LA FOLIE - FLIXECOURT. DOMQUEUR	BELLOY-sur-SOMME.	Head not to pass X-roads at LA FOLIE till tail of the fighting troops 7th Bde has passed.
H.Q. R.H.A. Field Sqn. Div. Amm. Col. under orders of C.R.H.A.	CONTEVILLE.	10-30 am. 10-32 am. 10-45 am.	D of DOMLEGER - Ain- do CRAMONT - AILSON- ROLLAND - thence follow the 3rd Signal Sqn. DOMQUEUR-ST.OUEN	BELLOY-sur-SOMME.	Head not to pass Ain. do CRAMONT till tail of 3rd Signal Sqn. is clear.
No.7 L.A.M. Car Battery.	NEUILLY-l'HOPITAL.	—	YVRENCH - ST.OUEN - FLIXECOURT.	BELLOY-sur-SOMME.	(a) To clear YVRENCH by 9-30 am. (b) To clear FLIXECOURT by 11 a.m.

Appendix IV

GENERAL STAFF No. G. 377/9. 3rd CAVALRY DIVISION

6th Cavalry Brigade.
7th Cavalry Brigade.
8th Cavalry Brigade.
C.R.H.A.
3rd Field Squadron R.E.
3rd Signal Squadron R.E.
No. 7 L.A.C. Battery.
Divnl. Ammunition Column.
O.C. A.S.C.
A.D.M.S.
A.D.V.S.

A.P.M.
Anti-gas Instructor.
D.A.D.O.S.
Liaison Officer.
Camp Commandant.
A.D.C.
A.A. & Q.M.G.
Chaplain.
Field Cashier.
Cavalry Corps (for information).
Fourth Army. (for information).
Xth Corps. (for information).

---

1. The Division will march tomorrow, September 14th, from present billeting area to "X" area, (North & South of BUSSY-les-DAOURS), now occupied by the 2nd Indian Cavalry Division, in accordance with March Table overleaf.

2. (a) "B" Echelons will be Divisionalised under orders of the Senior Brigade Transport Officer.
   (b) The following units will move under orders to be issued by the A.A. & Q.M.G.:-

   Ammunition Park.
   12th Sanitary Section.
   Reserve Park.

   (c) Motor Ambulances under orders of A.D.M.S., and No. 7 L.A.C. Battery, will move independently so as to clear the Eastern end of AMIENS by 1.30 p.m. Route:- Northern outskirts of AMIENS, thence along the AMIENS - VECQUEMONT road. They will not enter their billeting area in VECQUEMONT till they get orders to do so.

3. Divisional H.Q. will move to VECQUEMONT after 2 p.m.

4. Acknowledge.

13/9/1916.

A. Paget
Lieut-Colonel.
G.S. 3rd Cavalry Division.

MARCH TABLE - 3rd CAVALRY DIVISION - September 14th 1916.

Unit.	Starting Pt.	Time.	Route.	
8th Brigade.	E. end of ARGOEUVES.	7 am.	N. outskirts AMIENS - RIVERY - CAMON.	Brigade will water just W. of LAMOTTE; after watering will move direct via LAMOTTE, past T-roads 1 mile N. of LAMOTTE to a suitable off-saddling place W. of their eventual bivouacs which will be in valley about ½ mile S. of QUERRIEU.
6th Brigade.	W. end of ST. SAUVEUR.	8 am.	Follow the 8th Brigade.	Will water after 8th Brigade and proceed as above and halt W. of their bivouacking area which is N. of BUSSY.
7th Brigade.	W. end of BELLOY.	8-15 am.	Follow the 6th Brigade.	Will water after 6th Brigade and proceed as above, halting W. of their bivouacking area, which is S.E. of BUSSY.
H.Q., R.H.A. Dvl. H.Q. details. Signal Sqn. Field Sqn. Ammunition Col.	E. end of BELLOY.	9 am. 9-5 am. 9-10 am. 9-15 am. 9-30 am.	Follow the 7th Brigade.	These units will not form up on road till 7th Brigade is clear of BELLOY. Will water after 7th Brigade and proceed thence via E. of LAMOTTE to bivouacs about the Q of VECQUEMONT.
'B' Echelons in order of march of Bdes. under senior Bde. Transport Officer.				Divisional Troops 'B' Echelon will follow the Dvl. Amn. Col. from BELLOY about 9-45 am. The 7th Brigade will follow the Divisional Troops from BELLOY, the 6th and 8th will join in respectively at LA CHAUSSEE and ARGOEUVES behind Dvl. Troops, so that the eventual order of 'B' Echelons will be - Dvl. Troops, 8th, 6th, 7th. After watering W. of LAMOTTE, they will follow the Dvl. Ammunition Column to the Q of VECQUEMONT and rejoin their Brigades in X area bivouacs so soon as a Divisional Staff Officer reports the road to BUSSY clear.

NOTE - Before watering all units will close up into mass formation close to watering place, so as not to block those in rear. All units will be E. of CAMON by 2 p.m.

Appendix V.
W.D.

6th Cavalry Bde.	A.P.M.
7th Cavalry Bde.	D.A.D.O.S.
8th Cavalry Bde.	Anti-Gas Instructor.
C.R.H.A.	Liaison Officer.
3rd Field Sqn. R.E.	Field Cashier.
3rd Signal Sqn.	Chaplain.
No.7 L.A. Cars.	A.D.C.
Divl. Amm. Column.	Camp Commandant.
O.C. A.S.C.	A.A. & Q.M.G.
A.D.M.S.	Cavalry Corps) for
A.D.V.S.	Fourth Army) information.

General Staff, No. G.410/1, 3rd Cavalry Division

---

1.   The Division will move to a position of readiness at BONNAY and LA NEUVILLE tomorrow, September 15th, in accordance with attached March Table.

2.   The Division will move on 'B' Scale as amended in 3 C.D. No.4932 of 12th instant, but the following will remain under the orders of the O.C. A.S.C. in X area bivouacs and come under the orders of the Cavalry Corps for movements.

   (a) G.S. wagons of the Divisional Ammunition Column.
   (b) 'B' Echelon wagons of Brigades and Divisional Troops.
   (c) Auxiliary Horsed Transport Company.
   (d) Ammunition Park.
   (e) 12th Sanitary Section.
   (f) Any dismounted details not employed with working parties.

Note - Divisional and Brigade motor cars will eventually be sent back to X area to report to O.C. A.S.C.

3.   (a) With reference to para. 2 (a), the S.A.A. Mobile Section of the Divisional Ammunition Column will accompany the Division.

   (b) Mobile Veterinary Sections will be collected by and march under the orders of the A.D.V.S., who will be responsible for informing Brigades and Divisional Troops of their eventual location, when the Division gets east of the MARICOURT - FRICOURT road.

   (c) Field Ambulances will be disposed as follows :-
        Mobile Sections with Brigades.
        Heavy Sections divisionalised under orders of the A.D.M.S.   Heavy Sections will include the G.S. wagons of the Field Ambulances and all Motor Ambulances.

   (d) Batteries and 'A' Echelons will accompany their Brigades.

4.   The G.S. wagons of the Divisional Ammunition Column and the Auxiliary Horsed Transport Company attached to them and carrying ammunition, will be collected just south of the T of VECQUEMONT under the direction of the O.C. Divisional Ammunition Column, so soon as the Division moves forward from present area.
   This column will be moved forward under the orders of the Cavalry Corps, who will inform the Division.

5.

2.

5. The Division will move via DAOURS and eventually form two columns at BONNAY and LA NEUVILLE respectively at 11 a.m.
The BONNAY column will consist of the 7th and 6th Brigades.
The LA NEUVILLE " " " " " 8th & Divl. Troops.

Both columns will be massed off the road north of the river in such a position that they can cross to the south bank at both places at short notice.

After 11 a.m., Brigades must be prepared to move south of the river at half-an-hour's notice after receipt of orders at Brigade Headquarters.

A Divisional Staff Officer will meet representatives from Brigades and Divisional Troops at the northern exits of BONNAY and LA NEUVILLE respectively at 8 a.m. to point out suitable bivouac areas.

6. The 7th and 8th Brigades respectively will tomorrow send an officer to reconnoitre routes across country to TREUX, between the CORBIE - BRAY and CORBIE - TREUX roads.

The Officer from the 7th Brigade taking a northern route.
" " " " 8th " " " southern "

7. Divisional Headquarters will remain at the Mairie, VECQUEMONT, till the Division moves forward from BONNAY and LA NEUVILLE.

8. Acknowledge.

Lieutenant-Colonel,
General Staff,
14/9/16. 3rd Cavalry Division.

MARCH TABLE - 3rd Cavalry Division - 15/9/16.

Unit.	Starting Point.	Time.	Route.	Assembly area.	Remarks.
7th Cavalry Bde.	T-roads 200 yards N. of T in VECQUEMONT.	7-15 am.	Q of DAOURS - track leaving the DAOURS - LA NEUVILLE Road S.E. of Hill 80 leading to Q of BONNAY.	S. and W. of BONNAY.	
6th Cavalry Bde.	ditto.	8 am.	ditto.	ditto.	To follow 7th Brigade.
8th Cavalry Bde.	ditto.	8-45 am.	Q of DAOURS to LA NEUVILLE.	W. and N.W. of LA NEUVILLE.	
Dvl. H.Q. details.	ditto.	9-30 am.	ditto.	ditto.	To follow 8th Brigade.
CRHA. S.Sqn.	ditto.	9-35 am.	ditto.	ditto.	
Fd. Sqr.	ditto.	9-40 am.	ditto.	ditto.	
Amm. Col. (less Heavy Sect)	ditto.	9-50 a.m.	ditto.	ditto.	
Divisionalised Fd. Ambces less Mob. Sects.	ditto.	10 a.m.	ditto.	ditto.	
		10-15 am.		ditto.	A.D.M.S. will arrange to collect all Field Ambces. at the Starting Point. D.V.S. will arrange to collect all Mobile Vet. Sects. at the Starting Pt.
Divisionalised Mobile Vet. Sects.	ditto.	10-25 am.	ditto.	ditto.	
No.7 L.A.Cars.	ditto.	10-40 am.	ditto.	W. entrance to LA NEUVILLE.	

SECRET
WAR DIARY

G.416/2.
Appendix VI

6th Cavalry Bde.
7th Cavalry Bde.
8th Cavalry Bde.
C.R.H.A.
3rd Field Sqn. R.E.
3rd Signal Sqn.

Ref. 1/40,000.

1. An attack is being launched today by Fourth Army in conjunction with the French and Reserve Army. The objective of the Fourth Army is the line MORVAL - LESBOEUFS - GUEDECOURT - FLERS.

2. If the attack of the Fourth Army succeeds in gaining the above objectives, the Cavalry will advance with the following objectives :-
   (a) 1st Cavalry Division - (moving N. of LEUZE WOOD) ROCQUIGNY - BARASTRE.
   (b) 2nd Indian Cavalry Division - (moving E. of DELVILLE WOOD) VILLERS-au-FLOS - BANCOURT.
   (c) 2nd Cavalry Division - (moving W. of LONGUEVAL) BAPAUME and the ground N. of it.

3. The 1st Indian and 3rd British Cavalry Divisions will be in reserve - the former about DERNANCOURT.
   These Divisions will not move forward until the MAMETZ and CARNOY areas are vacated by the 2nd Indian, 2nd and 1st British Cavalry Dvns.

4. The following localities will be kept under fire by the Corps Heavy Artillery - LE TRANSLOY - BEAULENCOURT - BARASTRE - VILLERS-au-FLOS - RIENCOURT - BAUCOURT.
   Fire will not be lifted from LE TRANSLOY and BEAULENCOURT, but guns will stop firing on the other 4 villages as soon as Cavalry are reported E. of the PERONNE - BAPAUME road.

5. Green flares will be used by the Cavalry, Red by the Infantry, to help aeroplanes locate our troops.

6. Water will be practically unobtainable after leaving either the CARNOY or MAMETZ areas.

7. Should the Division move forward from LA NEUVILLE and BONNAY, it will probably do so in 2 columns across country: 7th followed by the 6th S. of TREUX, 8th followed by Divl. Troops N. of MORLANCOURT.
   After passing these places, routes will probably be via the tracks previously reconnoitred by Brigades last July, viz: through F.26, 27 and 28, thence via F.22. and 15 to MAMETZ or via F.29. and 24 to CARNOY.
   Consequently the 7th and 8th Brigades respectively must be prepared to send on officers to reconnoitre these tracks, after orders to advance are received.
   These tracks, on the original tracing given to Brigades, were marked 'A' and 'B'.

8. Brigades will water so soon as possible after arriving N. of BONNAY and LA NEUVILLE.

9. These orders are only preparatory - more detailed orders will be issued should the Division move further east.

10. Divisional Headquarters will remain at the Mairie, VECQUEMONT, till the Division moves east.

11. Acknowledge.

Sgd/ A.E. PAGET, Lieutenant-Colonel,
General Staff,
3rd Cavalry Division.

15/9/16.

Appendix VII.

G.416/12.

6th Cavalry Bde.	A.P.M.
7th Cavalry Bde.	D.A.D.O.S.
8th Cavalry Bde.	Anti-Gas Instructor.
C.R.H.A.	Liaison Officer.
3rd Field Sqn.	Field Cashier.
3rd Signal Sqn.	Chaplain.
No.7 L.A. Cars.	A.D.C.
Ammunition Col.	Camp Commandant.
O.C. A.S.C.	A.A & Q.M.G.
A.D.M.S.	Cavalry Corps (for information.)
A.D.V.S.	

1. The Division will march to fresh bivouacs tomorrow 17th September, so as to be clear of the PONT NOYELLES - DAOURS road by 8-45 a.m. as follows :-
   (a) <u>7th Brigade</u> across country keeping north of BOIS ESCARDONNEUSE to bivouac just south of PONT NOYELLES leaving 7 a.m.
   (b) <u>6th Brigade</u> across country keeping south of the BOIS ESCARDONNEUSE to bivouac half-a-mile south of PONT NOYELLES, leaving 7 a.m.
   (c) <u>8th Brigade</u> via Q of DAOURS to bivouac south of VECQUEMONT leaving 7 a.m.
   (d) <u>Divisional Troops</u> in following order of march :-
      Divisionalised Mobile Veterinary Sections.
      " Cavalry Field Ambulances.
      Ammunition Column. (less G.S. Wagons).
      Field Squadron.
      Signal Squadron.
      Headquarters, R.H.A.
will follow 8th Brigade, head of Mobile Veterinary Sections to leave about 7-30 a.m.
   Route - Q of DAOURS, thence road to PONT NOYELLES till opposite bivouacking area, north-east of BUSSY.
   (e) <u>No.7 Light Armoured Car Battery</u> will precede head of 8th Brigade to previous bivouac in VECQUEMONT.

2. (a) 'B' Echelons of 6th and 7th Brigades will march independently via QUERRIEU and PONT NOYELLES so as to join their Brigades in new bivouacs south of PONT NOYELLES by 8-45 a.m.
   (b) Divisional Troops 'B' Echelon will receive separate orders to rejoin their units from A.A & Q.M.G.
   (c) 'B' Echelon 8th Brigade will march via BUSSY to VECQUEMONT to rejoin Brigade in fresh bivouac by 8-45 a.m.

3. Brigades will strike tents and leave them ready packed as follows :-
   6th and 7th Brigades alongside the road from LA NEUVILLE to A of BONNAY.
   8th Brigade and Divisional Troops alongside the DAOURS - LA NEUVILLE road.
   A guard of 1 N.C.O. and 2 men per Brigade will remain with them till 8-30 a.m. when lorries will fetch them.

4. Staff Captains will meet Divisional Staff Officers as follows :-
   6th and 7th Brigades also representatives of Divisional Troops at the X-roads south of P of PONT NOYELLES at 7-30 a.m.
   Staff Captain 8th Brigade at Church at DAOURS at 7-30 a.m.

5. Divisional Headquarters will remain at the Mairie, VECQUEMONT.
6. Acknowledge.

11-45 p.m.
16/9/18.

Lieutenant-Colonel,
G.S. 3rd Cavalry Division.

Appendix VIII.

General Staff No. G.434/1. 3rd Cavalry Division

6th Cavalry Bde.	D.A.D.O.S.
7th Cavalry Bde.	Anti-Gas Instructor.
8th Cavalry Bde.	Liaison Officer.
C.R.H.A.	Field Cashier.
3rd Field Sqn.	Chaplain.
3rd Signal Sqn.	A.D.C.
No.7 L.A. Cars.	Camp Commandant.
Dvl. Ammunition Col.	A.A & Q.M.G.
O.C. A.S.C.	Brigade Transport Officer,
A.D.M.S.	7th Cavalry Bde.
A.D.V.S.	Cavalry Corps. (for information).
A.P.M.	X Corps (for information).

1. The Division will march tomorrow, September 22nd, to a billeting area west of AMIENS between BOUCHON and ST.PIERRE-a-GOUY, in accordance with attached March Table.

2. (a) Brigades will march at the rate of 5 miles per hour.
   (b) 'B' Echelons will be divisionalised and march under orders of 7th Brigade Transport Officer.
   (c) Brigades will be accompanied by their Mobile Veterinary Sections and Field Ambulances complete.
   Mobile Sections of the Divisional Ammunition Column will march with Batteries.
   (d) A.D.M.S. will issue orders for the move of all Motor Ambulances.

3. The following units will move under separate orders to be issued by the A.A. & Q.M.G. :-

   Ammunition Park.
   Reserve Park.
   Auxiliary Horse Transport Company.
   12th Sanitary Section.
   Dismounted party.

4. Divisional Headquarters will move to LE QUESNOY after 12 noon.

5. Acknowledge.

Lieutenant-Colonel,
General Staff,
3rd Cavalry Division.

21/9/1916.

MARCH TABLE, 3rd CAVALRY DIVISION - 22nd September 1916.

Unit.	Starting Pt.	Time.	Route.	Billeting Area.	Remarks.
8th Brigade.	X-roads just N. of the N of VECQUEMONT.	9 am.	LAMOTTE - CAMON - AMIENS Stn. - AILLY - PICQUIGNY.	BOUCHON - L'ETOILE.	Keeping S. of the SOMME all the way as far as CONDÉ.
7th Brigade.	ditto.	10-45 am	ditto.	CONDÉ - FOLIE - HANGEST.	Follow the 8th Bde.
8th Brigade.	ditto.	12.30 pm	ditto.	SOUES - LE MESGE.	Will turn off the main road at PICQUIGNY.
Div. H.Q. Details 3rd Sig. Sqdn. } under orders of O.C. 3rd Signal Sqdn.	ditto.	1.30 pm 1.35 pm	ditto.	LE QUESNOY.	Will follow the 6th Bde.
H.Q. R.H.A. Div. Ammn. Col. }	ditto.	1.45 pm.	ditto.	CROUY.	
3rd Fd. Sqdn.	ditto.	2.5. pm.	ditto.	LE GARD.	
'B' Echelons in order of march of Bdes. & Divl. Troops under orders of 7th Bde. Transport Officer.	ditto.	2-20 pm	ditto.	ST.PIERRE-&-GOUY.	(a) 7th Bde. T.O. will arrange to collect the 'B' Echs. at the S.P. in the order 8th, 7th, 6th, Divl. Troops. (b) 'B' Echs. will billet as a unit for night of 22nd/23rd. A.A & Q.M.G. will arrange rations accordingly.
No.7 L.A.Car Battery.	ditto.	4-30 pm.	ditto.	CROUY.	

Appendix IX.

G.434/2.

8th Cavalry Bde.	A.P.M.
7th Cavalry Bde.	D.A.D.O.S.
8th Cavalry Bde.	Anti-Gas Instructor.
C.R.H.A.	Liaison Officer.
3rd Field Sqn.	Field Cashier.
3rd Signal Sqn.	Chaplain.
No.7 L.A.Car Battery.	A.D.C.
Div. Amm. Col.	Camp Commandant.
O.C. A.S.C.	A.A. & Q.M.G.
A.D.M.S.	Bde. Transport Offr,
A.D.V.S.	7th Cav.Bde.

Third Army)
Cavalry Corps)) for information.
X Corps)

---

1. The Division will march tomorrow, September 23rd, to a billeting area between the AUTHIE and CANCHE Rivers in accordance with the attached March Table.

2. The following will move under separate orders to be issued by the A.A & Q.M.G. :-

    Ammunition Park.
    No.12 Sanitary Section.
    Dismounted party.

The Reserve Park and Auxiliary Horse Transport Company will remain as at present located in Fourth Army area.

3. Heads of the 8th and 7th Cavalry Brigades will not cross the DOULLENS - AUXI-le-CHATEAU road before 12 noon.

4. Divisional Headquarters will move to FROHEN-le-GRAND.

5. Acknowledge.

                                    Sd/ A.E. PAGET, Lieutenant-Colonel,
                                                 General Staff,
                                                 3rd Cavalry Division.

22/9/16.

MARCH TABLE, 3rd CAVALRY DIVISION - 23rd September 1916.

Unit.	Starting Pt.	Time.	Route.	Billeting Area.	Remarks.
8th Brigade.	VAUCHELLES-les-DOMART.	9 am.	BRUCAMPS - DOMQUEUR - CRAMONT - CONTEVILLE - AUXI-le-CHATEAU - BUIRE.	FILLIEVRES - AUBROMETZ - MONCHEL - CONCHY-sur-CANCHE - ROUGEFAY.	Head not to cross DOULLENS - AUXI-le-CHATEAU road before 12 noon.
7th Brigade.	X-roads by Church in L'ETOILE.	9-45 am.	LA FOLIE - DOMART - PONTHIEU - BERNAVILLE - FROHEN-le-GRAND.	BOUBERS-sur-CANCHE - VACQUERIE-le-BOURCQ - BOFFLES - FORTEL - BONNIERES.	
6th Brigade.	HANGEST.	10-15 am.	FLIXECOURT - cross to N. bank of river - HALTE (N. of ST.OUEN) - W. end of DOMART - en-PONTHIEU - PROUVILLE.	BACHIMONT - BUIRE - NOEUX - WAVANS - BEAUVOIR RIVIERE - BEALCOURT - ST. ACHEUL.	Head not to cross DOMART en-PONTHIEU - BRUCAMPS road till tail of 7th Brigade has passed.
Dvl.H.Q. details & 3rd S.Sqn. under O.C. Sig. Sqn.	LE QUESNOY.	10-0 am.	HANGEST - BOURDON - FLIXECOURT - thence N. of the river - HALTE (N. of ST.OUEN) - DOMART -en-PONTHIEU - BERNAVILLE	FROHEN-le-GRAND.	Not to pass HANGEST Church till tail of 6th Brigade has passed.
H.Q. R.H.A. Div. Amm. Col.	HANGEST.	11-0 am.	Follow the 3rd Signal Sqn.	FROHEN-le-GRAND.	
3rd Field Sqn.	"	11-20 am.	Follow the D.A.Col.	FROHEN-le-PETIT.	
'B' Echs. under orders of 7th Bde. Transport Officer.	"	11-30 am.	Follow the 3rd Field Sqn.	"	
No.7 L.A.Cars.	CROUY.	-	Same as for 3rd Signal Sqn.	VILLERS-l'HOPITAL.	To move independently, so as to clear DOMART by 10-30 am. and not pass through FROHEN-le-GRAND before 12 noon.

Appendix F.

G.434/3.

```
6th Cavalry Bde.    Anti-Gas Instructor.
7th Cavalry Bde.    Liaison Officer.
8th Cavalry Bde.    Field Cashier.
C.R.H.A.            Chaplain.
3rd Field Sqn.      A.D.C.
3rd Signal Sqn.     Camp Commandant.
No.7 L.A.Cars.      AA. & Q.M.G.
Div. Amm. Col.      Brigade Transport Officer,
O.C. A.S.C.             7th Cav. Bde.
A.D.M.S.            Supply Column.
A.D.V.S.            Third Army      )
A.P.M.              Cavalry Corps   ) for information.
D.A.D.O.S.          G.H.Q. Troops   )
```
----

1. The Division will march tomorrow, September 24th, to a billeting area west of the HESDIN - LABROYE road, in accordance with attached March Table.

2. The following will move under separate orders to be issued by A.A & Q.M.G. :-

        Ammunition Park.
        12th Sanitary Section.

3. Mobile Sections of the Ammunition Column will remain with their Batteries for night 24th/25th, and rejoin the Ammunition Column on 25th instant.
    'B' Echelons will rejoin their units on the night 24th, vide March Table.

4. Troops of the 6th Brigade and Divisional Troops will be clear of the FROHEN-le-GRAND - AUXI-le-CHÂTEAU road by 8-30 a.m.

5. Divisional Headquarters will move to LE FOND DE MOURIEZ CHATEAU, 1 mile south of M of HARCONELLE.

6. Acknowledge.

23/9/16.

                            Lieutenant-Colonel,
                            General Staff,
                            3rd Cavalry Division.

MARCH TABLE, 3rd CAVALRY DIVISION – 24th September 1916.

Unit.	Starting Pt.	Time.	Route.	Billeting Area.	Remarks.
8th Brigade.	GALAMETZ.	8-30 am.	GALAMETZ – Ste. AUSTREBERTHE – MARCONELLE – HARESQUEL.	S. of River CANCHE. PLUMOISON – BOUIN – AUBIN ST.VAAST – BOQUEMICOURT – MARESQUEL – BEAURAINVILLE – LESPINOY – BOIS JEAN – CHATEAU ROMONT – LA NEUVILLE – LABEUS.	(a) The Bde will be W. of AUXI-le-CHATEAU by 8-30 am. – No troops may use the AUXI – FROHEN-le-GRAND road after that hour. (b) TORTEFONTAINE & GOUY-ST.ANDRE & CAMPAGNE-lez-HESDIN are not to be used for billets.
6th Brigade.	Under Bde. arrangements.		LE PONCHEL – LABROYE.	RAYE-sur-AUTHIE – FOND-de-VAL – DOURIEZ – ST.JOSSE – SAULCHOY – ST.REMY-aux-BOIS – MAINTENAY – ROUSSENT – BUIRE-le-SEC – LA HOUSSOYE.	
7th Brigade.	Forked road 500 yds. N. of LL of Pt. FILLIEVRES.	9-30 am.	GALAMETZ – HESDIN – GUISY – ST.VAAST.	N. of River CANCHE. CAVRON-ST.MARTIN – CONTES – LE PETIT BEAURAIN – LOISON-sur-CREQUOISE – MARENLA – AIX-en-ISSART – ST.DENOEUX – HESMOND – OFFIN.	

H.Q. R.H.A.

March Table continued.

Unit.	Starting Pt.	Time.	Route.	Billeting Area.	Remarks.
C.R.H.A. } Div. Amm. Col. }	VILLERS- l'HOPITAL.	8 am.	BOFFLES - ROUGEFAY - BACHIMONT - HARAVESNES - ERQUIERES - LE QUESNOY - CAPELLE.	MOURIEZ.	
3rd Field Sqn.	ditto.	8-20 am.	ditto.	ditto.	Must clear FROHEN-le-GRAND by 8 am.
Div.H.Q.details) 3rd Signal Sqn.) under O.C. Signal Sqn. }	ditto.	8-30 am.	ditto.	Neighbourhood of BREVILLERS.	Detailed billets will be allotted on reaching road junction B of BRAILLY.
'B' Echelons.				Under Bde. arrangements.	
'B' Echelon, 6th Brigade.	FROHEN-le-GRAND Church.	6-30 am.	WAVANS - AUXI-le-CHATEAU.		Will come under orders of 8th Bde. on reaching AUXI at 8 am. Cross to N. of CANCHE at AUBIN-ST.VAAST, where it will come under orders of 7th Bde.
'B' Echelon, 7th Brigade.	S. end of VILLERS-l'HOPITAL.	8-40 am.	VILLERS- l'HOPITAL - BOFFLES - ROUGEFAY - BACHIMONT - HARAVESNES - ERQUIERES - LE QUESNOY - PLUMOISON.		
'B' Echelon, 8th Brigade.	ditto.	8-50 am.	Follow 7th Bde. 'B' Echelon to PLUMOISON.		(a) To come under orders of 8th Bde. on reaching PLUMOISON. (b) Must be clear of FROHEN-le-GRAND by 8-30 am.
No.7 L.A.Cars.	ditto.	7-45 am.	BOFFLES - BUIRE - QUOEUX - FONTAINE.	-	Will await orders at REGNAUVILLE re billets.

Appendix 1.   G.444/12.

7th Cav.Bde.   6th Cav. Bde.   )
8th Cav.Bde.   Cavalry Corps.   ) for
A.D.M.S.   II Corps.   ) information.
O.C. Dismtd.Party.
A.A & Q.M.G.

Reference my G.444/11 of the 18th instant.

1. The H.Q. of the Dismounted Party, now employed on work under the Reserve Army, will be relieved on November 1st as follows :-

Commanding Officer........By a Major from 8th Bde.
Adjutant..................By a suitable officer from 7th Bde.
Q.M....................... "   "   "   " 8th "
R.S.M.....................By a senior Sergeant from 7th Bde.
R.Q.M.S................... "   "   "   " 8th "

The medical officer and medical personnel will be relieved under arrangements to be made by the A.D.M.S.

2. A motor car for the 3 officers and a light lorry for the N.C.O's, servants and kit will be at the most easterly road junction in AUBIN-ST.VAAST at 9 a.m. November 1st to pick up the H.Q. personnel above mentioned.

Medical personnel will move independently.

3. As soon as the relieving Commanding Officer has taken over to his satisfaction, the present H.Q. will return to Divisional billeting area.

7th and 8th Brigades should arrange to have necessary transport to meet their personnel relieved (vide my G.444/1) at same rendezvous (AUBIN-ST.VAAST) at 6 p.m. 1st November.

The 6th Brigade personnel will be conveyed back to the Brigade area by the motors bringing the party back.

4. N.C.O's and servants should take current day's rations with them.

5. H.Q. Dismounted Party are in camp at W.14.b.2.8. just E. of BOUZINCOURT.

                                    Sd/ A.E.PAGET, Lieut-Colonel,
29/10/16.   G.S. 3rd Cavalry Division.

Appendix 2.

SUBJECT :- <u>Divisional School of Instruction.</u>

```
6th Cavalry Bde.  20.    Capt.Hon.C.ANNESLEY,
7th Cavalry Bde.  20.      Royal Dragoons.
8th Cavalry Bde.  20.    Maj. T.C.GURNEY, DSO,
C.R.H.A.           1.      2nd Life Gds.            1.
3rd Field Sqn.     3.    Maj.E. de BURGH, DSO,
3rd Signal Sqn.    3.      General Staff.           1.
No.7 L.A. Cars.    1.    Capt.E.W.S.BALFOUR,DSO,
A.D.M.S.           1.      B.M., 7th Cav.Bde.       1.
A.D.V.S.           1.    Maj.F.KING, 6th M.G.Sqn.   1.
A.A & Q.M.G.       1.    Capt.J.B.WALKER, A.V.C.,
Maj.H.A.TOMKINSON,         2nd Life Guards.         1.
  Royal Dragoons.  1.    Cav. Corps (for inf).      1.
```

In continuation of my G.488 of the 15th instant.

1. A Divisional School of Instruction will open at MERLIMONT PLAGE on or as soon after November 6th as possible.

2. The Staff will be composed as follows :-

Commandant.....................Major H.A.TOMKINSON, R.Dragoons.
Adjutant.......................Capt.Hon.C.ANNESLEY,   "

Instructors (Resident)......Major T.C.GURNEY, D.S.O., 2nd L.G.
      "   "   ......Major E.de BURGH, D.S.O., G.S.
      "   "   ......Capt. E.W.S.BALFOUR, D.S.O.,
                                  Bde.Major, 7th Cav.Bde.

Instructors (Non-Resident)..Major F.KING, 4th Hrs., 6th M.G.Sqn.
      "   "   ..Capt. J.B.WALKER, A.V.C., 2nd L.G.

3. The above Staff will instruct in the subjects as shown against their names :-

<u>The Commandant</u>   - 1. <u>Horsemastership.</u>

    (a) In billets.
    (b) In bivouacs.
    (c) On the march.
    (d) Saddle-fitting.
    (e) Packsaddlery.
    (f) Prevention and cure of galls, rubs, brushing, forging, corns, etc.

   2. <u>Equitation.</u>

    Training men to ride over, and horses to jump, trenches, ditches, shell holes, banks.

<u>Major T.C.GURNEY</u>   - <u>Cavalry Tactics.</u>

    (a) Tactics in the Attack, mounted.
    (b)   "   " "   "   , dismounted.
    (c) Combination of rifle and shock action in the Attack.
    (d) Combination of Cavalry, Artillery and Machine Guns.
    (e) Attack and defence of localities.

-2-

          (f) Siting and marking out trenches.
          (g) Capturing and using or destroying
              hostile guns.
          (h) Forcing passage of rivers and defiles.
          (j) Forming bridgeheads and holding them.
          (k) Seizing and holding positions in
              advance of infantry.

Major E. de BURGH.   - Training as Instructors.
                             (System of Progressive Training).

          (a) Teaching map-reading and reporting.
          (b) Preparing schemes.
          (c) Lecturing.
          (d) Discipline :-
              (i) Method of giving orders.
             (ii) Manners with subordinates.
            (iii) Care of men's health & comfort.
          (e) Methods of Instruction - on map and
              ground - Use of sand tables and
              squared cloth - Small tactical
              exercises on sand table or map.

Capt. E.W.S. BALFOUR.   - Training as Leaders.

     1.   Protection at the Halt.
          (a) Billets.
          (b) Bivouacs.
          (c) March outposts.

     2.   Protection on the Move.
          (a) Advance Guards.
          (b) Flank Guards.
          (c) Rear Guards.

     3.   Reconnaissance.
          (a) Protective Reconnaissance.
          (b) Independent reconnoitring
              detachments.

Major F. KING.   - Machine Guns and Hotchkiss Rifles.

          (a) The use of Machine Guns in attack
              and defence.
          (b) The use of Hotchkiss Rifles in
              attack and defence.

Captain J.B. WALKER.   - Shoeing & Minor Ailments.

          (a) Preparation of the foot and fitting
              shoes (hot & cold). Special shoeing
              for brushing, stumbling & forging.
          (b) Detection and treatment of incipient
              ailments such as coughs, colds, lice,
              mange, constipation, diarrhoea, liver
              disorders, fever.

4.   The Courses will be :-

   (a) For Squadron Leaders - 2 weeks.

   (b) For Squadron 2nds-in-Command & subalterns - 4 weeks.

5. All officers attending the School will be required to bring with them :-

    (a) 2 servants & 2 horses.
        (their 3rd horse must be kept with their Squadrons).
    (b) Bedding.
    (c) Note books, maps (ABBEVILLE & LENS Sheets).

6. There will be at each course, 3 classes of 9 officers each (each class will consist of 1 officer from every Regiment in the Division).

Each class will mess together. The senior officer in each mess will be responsible for the discipline of his mess, and also for the looking after the furniture and crockery in the house. When he hands over to the next class he will hand over the inventory of furniture etc. - any furniture or crockery broken by the members of his mess will be paid for by the officers concerned, before they leave.

7. The Commandant will be responsible for the general discipline of the School.

8. Unless further orders are issued on the subject, it may be assumed that :-

    (a) The first course will be for Squadron Leaders. Consequently, every Squadron Leader in the Division will be prepared to assemble at the School any day after November 5th.

    (b) The second and subsequent courses will be for Squadron Seconds-in-Command and Subalterns.

Brigades will therefore arrange for regimental rosters to be prepared, and names submitted to Divisional Headquarters, when called for.

Note - No two officers in the same Squadron may attend the School at the same time.

9. It is pointed out that the short course for Squadron Leaders is being arranged purely to demonstrate to them the tactical training which their Seconds-in-Command and Subalterns will undergo during their months course, so that there will be a uniform system of training throughout the Division.

10. It is hoped that, from time to time, lectures will also be given by various officers in the Army, on Artillery, Infantry and other subjects, as was arranged last winter.

11. The A.D.M.S. will arrange for the necessary medical and sanitary supervision over the School.
    A Medical Officer should be available when called for.
    All arrangements will be made by the A.D.M.S. with the Adjutant of the School.

26/10/16.

Lieutenant-Colonel, G.S.
3rd Cavalry Division.

Appendix 3.

SUBJECT - Winter Training 1916 - 1917.

ANTI-GAS SCHOOL.

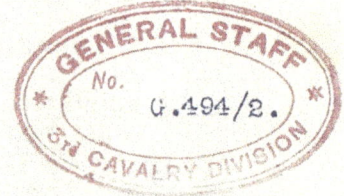

20.	6th Cavalry Brigade.	A.P.M.	1.
20.	7th Cavalry Brigade.	D.A.D.O.S.	1.
20.	8th Cavalry Brigade.	O.C. A.S.C.	1.
1.	C.R.H.A.	Chaplain.	1.
3.	3rd Field Sqn. R.E.	Anti-Gas Instructor.	4.
3.	3rd Signal Squadron.	Liaison Officer.	1.
3.	No.7 L.A.Cars.	A.A. & Q.M.G.	1.
1.	A.D.M.S.	Cavalry Corps (for information).	1.
1.	A.D.V.S.		

In continuation of my G.494 of the 21st instant.

1. A Divisional Anti-Gas School will be opened at the Château, 1 mile N.E. of WAILLY, on or about November 5th, with the object of training as many officers and N.C.O's as possible in Anti-Gas protection.

Those trained will subsequently act as Instructors to their Units, under direction of the Unit Commander.

2. The Commandant of the School will be Lieutenant E.G.WINDLE, Essex Yeomanry, Divisional Anti-Gas Instructor, who will be assisted by the following N.C.O's :-

Sergt. P.P.HARRIS, Leicestershire Yeomanry.
Sergt. H.COLEY, N. Somerset Yeomanry.
Corpl. F.PHELAN, Xth Royal Hussars.

These N.C.O's will be detached from their regiments until the School closes.

3. There will be two courses at the School :-

(a) For officers, lasting 3 days.
(b) "   N.C.O's,   "   5 "

Consequently, it will be possible to have, alternate weeks :-

2 classes of officers of 3 days each.
1 class of N.C.O's of 5 days.

A certain proportion of Officers and N.C.O's will be sent from every unit in the Division as opportunity offers but to commence with, and until further orders, they will be detailed as follows :-

Officers Course of 3 days :-

From each Brigade............2 officers - total 6.

N.B. Brigades will detail officers proportionately from each unit in the Brigade, so that by next March or so, each unit will have a proportion of officers trained in Anti-Gas measures.

N.C.O's

N.C.O's Course of 5 days :-

From each Brigade................4 N.C.O's - total 12.
"   Field Squadron...............1 N.C.O. -   "   1.
"   Signal Squadron..............1 N.C.O. -   "   1.
"   L.A. Car Battery.............1 N.C.O. -   "   1.
"   Ammunition Column............1 N.C.O. -   "   1.

                                                 "   16.

N.B. Brigades will detail their N.C.O's proportionately from each unit in the Brigade (see above).
N.C.O's may be of any rank.

4. Courses will assemble as follows :-

1st Week ...   ...   On Sunday afternoon - Class of Officers.
                     On Wednesday "   -   "   "   "

2nd Week ...   ...   On Sunday afternoon - Class of N.C.O's.

3rd Week ...   ...   On Sunday afternoon - Class of Officers.
                     On Wednesday "   -   "   "   "

4th Week ...   ...   On Sunday afternoon - Class of N.C.O's.

and so on ....

In the officers classes, it is important that officers of every rank should attend; G.H.Q. lays down that it is most important for Commanding Officers, Seconds-in-Command of Regiments, Adjutants and Squadron Leaders to have a thorough knowledge of Anti-Gas measures.
Consequently, senior officers should attend the early courses, followed in turn by the more junior officers, as they can be spared.

5. The A.D.M.S. will arrange that there is a Medical Officer on duty per week; he need not sleep at the School, but should attend during the day.
The Medical Officer detailed can at the same time benefit by the lectures and demonstrations.

6. The syllabus for the 5 days course for N.C.O's will be as follows :-

1st Day.....Lecture   - Gas Offensive and use of Smoke.
            (Introductory)
            Lecture   - Smoke Candles and Bombs.
            Practical - Smoke demonstration.
            Lecture   - Breathing - gas poisoning.
               "   - Tube Helmets, description, use, and
                           care of.

2nd Day.

2nd Day....Lecture   - Inspection of Helmets.
         Practical -   "   "   "
             "   - Wearing Helmets in Gas and
                        Lachrymatory Gas Clouds.
         Lecture   - Gas Shells.
             "   - Training men is use of Helmets.
         Practical - Helmet Drill - inspection of Helmets.

3rd Day....Lecture   - Small Box Respirator.
         Practical -   "   "   "
         Lecture   - Protection of Dug-outs from Cylinder
                        & Shell Gas.
         Practical - Helmet Drill.
         Lecture   - Vermorel and other Sprayers.
         Practical - Stripping and assembling above.

4th Day....Lecture   - Fitting S.B. Respirator.
         Practical - Testing same in Gas.
         Lecture   - Training in use of and inspection of
                        same.
         Practical - Drill.
         Lecture   - Clearing Dug-outs of Gas.
         Practical -   "   "   "   " " by fans and
                        fires.

5th Day....Lecture   - Wind observation, Gas Alarms and
                        "Gas Alert".
         Practical - Helmet & S.B. Respirator drill.
         Lecture   - Gas sampling - Tubes and Gas detection.
         Practical - Changing Helmets in Gas.
         Lecture   - Routine duties and gas duties of
                        Squadron N.C.O's.
         Practical - Test in Instruction.

The officers course will be a modified one on the above lines.

7.   (a) All officers will be accomodated in the Château, where a mess will be established.
         Officers should bring bedding.
         Each officer can bring 1 servant and 1 horse.
         Horses can be billeted in the Château grounds.

     (b) N.C.O's will be accomodated in a house in the Château grounds.
         A mess room will be provided.
         N.C.O's should bring blankets, mess tins, knife, fork, spoon, etc.
         N.C.O's horses cannot be billeted, consequently those who are within riding distance should ride over and send their horses back, arranging for them to be brought back at the termination of their course.
         Those N.C.O's who are too far away to ride, should be conveyed under arrangements to be made by the Brigade or Unit concerned.

-4-

8. Further orders will be issued with regard to the exact date when the School opens, but in the meanwhile Brigades and Divisional Troops should select officers and N.C.O's for the early courses (vide para. 3) and be prepared to send officers and N.C.O's weekly after the opening of the School.

9. Gas helmets need not be taken to the School, but will be provided there.

25th October 1916.

Lieutenant-Colonel,
General Staff,
3rd Cavalry Division.

appendix 4

Subject:- **Divisional Anti-Gas School.**　　　　　G.494/4.

6th Cavalry Brigade.	O.C.A.S.C.	Ammunition Column.
7th Cavalry Brigade.	A.D.M.S.	Ammunition Park.
8th Cavalry Brigade.	A.D.V.S.	Supply Column.
C.R.H.A.	A.P.M.	Aux: H.T. Company.
3rd Field Squadron R.E.	D.A.D.O.S.	No.12 Sanitary Sec.
3rd Signal Squadron.	Chaplain.	Anti-Gas Officer.
No. 7 L.A.C. Battery.	Liaison Officer.	Camp Commandant.
		A.A.& Q.M.G.

In continuation of my G.494/2 of the 25th instant:-

1. The Divisional Anti-Gas School will open at the Chateau, one mile N.E. of WAILLY on Sunday November 12th, on which date the first class will assemble; work commences the following day.

2. The 1st Course will be for N.C.O's, the following week there will be 2 Courses for officers, the 3rd week a N.C.O's Course, 4th week 2 Courses for officers, and so on.
   The attached Table of Courses will serve as a guide for all concerned.

3. Brigades and Divisional Troops concerned will detail N.C.O's to attend first course in accordance with attached Table and will submit names to Divisional Headquarters by midday November 10th.
   Unless further orders are issued on the subject, they will continue to submit names for every class 2 clear days before the class is due to assemble.
   N.C.O's will bring with them the current days' rations.
   Brigades & Divisional Troops will make their own arrangements about transport to and from the School.

4. All units are requested to read carefully the instructions given in my G.494/2 of the 25th, especially paras 3, 4 (latter part), 7 and 9.

5. 　Sergt. H.Coney   N.S.Y.　　　)
　　　　　and　　　　　　　　　　) will report to the Anti-Gas
　　Corpl F.Phelan 10th Rl Hrs.)
Officer at the Chateau, 1 mile N.E. of WAILLY, on the afternoon of the 8th instant as Assistant Instructors.

7/11/18.

　　　　　　　　　　　　　　　　　　　　　Lieutenant-Colonel.
　　　　　　　　　　　　　　　　　General Staff, 3rd Cavalry Division.

G.494/4.

COURSES AT ANTI-GAS SCHOOL.

N.B. Dates mentioned are the days the classes should arrive.

Date.	Course.	Class.	Detail.
Nov. 12.	1st Course.	N.C.O's.	4 per Brigade & 1 from each of the following:- Fd: Sqdn: L.A.C.Battery, Ammn: Col: Supply Col:
Nov. 19.	2nd Course.	Officers.	2 per Brigade.
Nov. 22.	3rd Course.	"	2 per Brigade.
Nov. 26.	4th Course.	N.C.O's.	As for 1st Course.
Dec. 3.	5th Course.	Officers.	As for 2nd Course.
Dec. 6.	6th Course.	"	-do-
Dec. 10.	7th Course.	N.C.O's.	As for 1st Course.
Dec. 17.	8th Course.	Officers.	As for 2nd Course.
Dec. 20.	9th Course.	"	-do-
Dec. 26.	10th Course.	N.C.O's.	As for 1st Course.
Dec. 31.	11th Course.	Officers.	As for 2nd Course.
Jan. 3.	12th Course.	"	-do-
Jan. 7.	13th Course.	N.C.O's.	4 per Brigade & 1 from each of the following:- Fd: Sqdn: Ammn: Col: Supply Col: Ammn. Park.
Jan. 14.	14th Course.	Officers.	2 per Brigade.
Jan. 17.	15th Course.	"	-do-
Jan. 21.	16th Course.	N.C.O's.	As for 13th Course.
Jan. 28.	17th Course.	Officers.	As for 14th Course.
Jan. 31.	18th Course.	"	-do-
Feb. 4.	19th Course.	N.C.O's.	As for 13th Course.
Feb. 11.	20th Course.	Officers.	As for 14th Course.
Feb. 14.	21st Course.	"	-do-

Feb. 18.

continued.

Date.	Course.	Class.	Detail.
Feb. 18.	22nd Course.	N.C.O's.	4 per Brigade & 1 from each of the following:- Fd: Sqdn: Ammn: Park. Aux: H.T.Coy. Sanitary Section.
Feb. 25.	23rd Course.	Officers.	2 per Brigade.
Feb. 28.	24th Course.	"	-do-
Mar. 4.	25th Course.	N.C.O's.	As for 22nd Course.
Mar. 11.	26th Course.	Officers.	As for 23rd Course.
Mar. 14.	27th Course.	"	-do-

The following units will arrange direct with the Anti-Gas Officer for the attendance of their Officers and N.C.O's at Courses when convenient to fit them in:
They will be additional to the numbers allotted and they will only attend daily, as no billets will be available:-

Signal Squadron.   ...   3 Officers 6 N.C.O's.
Supply Column.   ...   As many officers as can be spared.
Ammunition Col.   ...   2 Officers.
Ammunition Park.   ...   2 Officers.
Aux: H.T.Coy.   ...   1 Officer.
M.M.P.   ...   3 N.C.O's.
Div. H.Q.Details.   ...   4 N.C.O's (Camp Commandant to arrange).
H.Q. IVth Bde. R.H.A..   1 Officer & 2 N.C.O's.
H.Q. A.S.C.   ...   1 Officer.

SUBJECT :- Winter Training of Signal Services.

G.519.

6th Cavalry Brigade.
7th Cavalry Brigade.
8th Cavalry Brigade.
3rd Signal Squadron.
A.A & Q.M.G.

The following instructions for the further training of the Signal Services this Winter, with a view to having an adequate trained reserve by the Spring, are issued for the guidance of all concerned :-

A.   Instruction within Brigades.

1.   (a) Each Regiment will at once start training in Visual Signalling, Telephony and Line Work, the number of men necessary to ensure having an establishment of 2 officers and 30 O.R. by the Spring.

   (b) Each Signal Troop will also train all its mounted personnel in the above subjects.
   Motor Cyclists will, from time to time, carry out despatch riding schemes and be taught to find their way about the country by memorizing the map.

2.   Reserve Signalling Officers of Regiments should at once be trained regimentally in Visual Signalling until they have reached the standard of a Second Class Signaller, when they will do a course at Divisional Schools, vide 'B'.

3.   Brigade Signal Troop Officers will be responsible for supervising the training of all signallers within the Brigade.
   They will put all regimental signallers through classification tests as under :-
   Semaphore   ...   ...   10 words a minute.
   Morse flag   8   "   "   "
   Buzzer   ...   ...   10 "   "   "
   Lamp & Helio...   ...   8   "   "   "
   Until a man has been classified by the Brigade Signalling Officer as a First Class Signaller he will continue to attend Regimental Classes.
   When Regimental Signalling Schemes are arranged the Brigade Signalling Officer should attend when possible.

B.   Divisional Signalling Courses.

1.   For Regimental & Reserve Regimental Signalling Officers.
   Duration - 2 or 4 weeks, according to classification.
   Those officers in regiments, who have already attended a Divisional Course, will attend a refresher course for a fortnight, commencing November 21st.
   The beginners who have never attended a Divisional Course will attend for one month, at a date to be notified later.
   Subjects for instruction :-
   Theory of Telephony & Telegraphy.
   Office Working.
   Line laying and office wiring.
   Training as an Instructor in Signalling Schemes, & electricity lectures.

2.

-2-

2. For N.C.O's of Regiments and Machine Gun Squadrons, and for men likely to be promoted N.C.O's :-

<u>Duration 3 weeks.</u>
<u>Establishment per course</u> :-
    1 man per regiment in the Division.
    1 man from each Machine Gun Sqn. in turn, commencing with the 6th M.G. Sqn.

<u>Subjects for instruction</u> :-
    Map-reading with reference to Visual Signalling.
    Electro-magnetism & Telephony.
    Line work.
    Testing and care of instruments.
    Office working.

    <u>First Course - November 14th.</u> (Class assembles 13th).

3. The course for N.C.O's will be prolonged for an extra week or so, for the benefit of those selected for more advanced training in electricity.

Reference B.1. - The following officers will attend a fortnight's course commencing November 20th (assemble 19th)

<u>6th Brigade.</u>	...	2/Lt. M.J.CLERY, 3rd D.G.
		2/Lt. R.F.HEYWORTH-SAVAGE, Royals.
<u>7th Brigade.</u>	...	Lieut. S.R.F.SPICER, 1st L. Gds.
<u>8th Brigade.</u>	...	Lieut. C.W.D.BELL, Xth Hussars.

The following officers will attend a fortnight's course commencing December 4th (assemble 3rd) :-

<u>6th Brigade.</u>	...	2/Lt. M.C.BIGGS, N.S.Y.
<u>7th Brigade.</u>	...	Lieut. C.J.HENRY, Leic. Yeo.
<u>8th Brigade.</u>	...	2/Lt. Hon. G.S.DAWSON-DAMER, Xth Hrs.

Names of N.C.O's and men to attend B.2. will be sent to O.C. 3rd Signal Sqn. by Nov. 12th.

6/11/16.
                            Sd/ A.E.PAGET, Lieutenant-Colonel,
                                   G.S. 3rd Cavalry Division.

APPENDIX 6.   G.512/4.

7th Cavalry Brigade.
8th Cavalry Brigade.
3rd Field Squadron R.E.
A.D.M.S.
A.A & Q.M.G.

    In continuation of my G.512/2 of 9th instant, the 7th and 8th Brigades will each find a Pioneer Battalion in accordance with the War Establishment attached.

    These Battalions will be ready to leave their billetting areas on the 20th November.

    The A.DM.S. will arrange for the following medical personnel to accompany each Battalion:-

    1 R.A.M.C. Officer.
    1 " Staff Sergeant or Sergeant.
    18 stretcher bearers.

NOTE - The 7th and 8th Brigades will each detail 8 R.A.M.C. rank and file for sanitary duties.

    The 3rd Field Squadron R.E. will arrange for the following R.E. personnel to accompany each Battalion :-

    1 Officer & 2 riding horses.
    1 Staff Sergeant or Sergeant.
    18 Sappers.
    2 Batmen.

                                Sd/ A.E.PAGET, Lieut-Colonel,
                                                General Staff,
11/11/16.   3rd Cavalry Division.

Issued Nov. 10th '16.   Appendix 6.

War Establishment. — British Cav. Pioneer Bn.

~~Proposed~~

DETAIL	PERSONNEL								HORSES					Bicycles	Motor Cycles	Remarks
	Officers	Warrant Officers	Clerks	Staff-serjeants and serjeants	Artificers	Trumpeters	Rank and file	Total	Riding	Draught	Heavy Draught	Pack	Total			
H.Q. (excluding attached)	4	2	1	3	4		22	36	5	12	4		21	6		
" attached.	2			3			48	53	2				2			
3 companies.	21	3		30			708	762		36	12		48			
Total Battalion	27	5	1	36	4		778	851	7	48	16		71	6		

Composition in detail.

DETAIL	Officers	Warrant Officers	Clerks	Staff-serjeants and serjeants	Artificers	Trumpeters	Rank and file	Total	Riding	Draught	Heavy Draught	Pack	Total	Bicycles	Motor Cycles	Remarks
Headquarters.																
Lt-Col. or Major O.C.	1							1	1				1			
Major or Capt 2nd-in-C.	1							1	1				1			
Adjutant.	1							1	1				1			
Quartermaster.	1							1	1				1			
Sergeant-Major.		1						1								
Q.M.S.		1						1								
Orderly Room Sergt.				1				1								
" " Clerk.			1					1								
Transport Sergeant.				1				1	1				1			
Saddler.					1			1								
Farrier Corporal.					1			1								
Shoeing-Smiths.					2			2								
Drivers (Tpt.for vehicles)							7	7		12	4		16			
Batmen.							5	5								
Cook.							1	1								
Signallers.														6		
Sergeant.				1				1								
Corporal.							1	1								
Privates.							6	6								
Orderlies for M.O. (a).							2	2								(a) 1 drives Maltese cart.
Attached.																
R.A.M.C. (Sanitary Sect.)	*1			*1			8	10								*Detailed by A.D.M.S.
Stretcher bearers.							18	18								
Gas duties.							1	1								
Armourer Sergeant.				1				1								
Interpreter.							1	1								
Field Squadron R.E.)																Detailed by C.R.E.
Officer.)	1							1	2				2			
Sergeant.)				1				1								
Sappers.)							18	18								
Batmen.)							2	2								
	6	2	1	6	4		70	89	7	12	4		23	6		

War Establishment.

DETAIL	PERSONNEL								HORSES					Bicycles	Motor Cycles	Remarks
	Officers	Warrant Officers	Clerks	Staff-serjeants and serjeants	Artificers	Trumpeters	Rank and file	Total	Riding	Draught	Heavy Draught	Pack	Total			
Company of 6 platoons.																
Captain O.C.	1							1								
Subaltern.	6							6								
Coy. S.M.		1						1								
Coy. Q.M.S.				1				1								
Sergeants.				9				9								
Corporals.							15	15								
Privates.							204	204								
Drivers (Tpt. for vehicles)							8	8		12	4		16			
Batmen.							7	7								
Cooks.							2	2								
Total Company.	7	1		10			236	254		12	4		16			

Transport.

	Vehicles.	Drivers.		Riding	Draught	Heavy Draught	Pack	Total			
Headquarters.											
Carts Maltese.	1	1			2			2			
" officers mess	1	1			2			2			
" water	2	2			4			4			
Wagons lim. G.S.	1	2			4			4			
" G.S.	1	2			4			4			
Wagons lim. G.S.	6	12			24			24			
" G.S.	3	6				12		12			
Travelling kitchens or Wagons lim. G.S. for cooks.	3	6.			12			12			
Total.	18	32			48	16		64			

www.ingramcontent.com/pod-product-compliance
Lightning Source LLC
Chambersburg PA
CBHW081242170426
43191CB00034B/2010